"The Path to Corporate Nirvana is a useful read for both new team members and experienced executives who sense that there should be a better way to get things done."

FRED HASSAN
CHAIRMAN & CHIEF EXECUTIVE OFFICER
PHARMACIA CORPORATION

"Each reader will gain perspective on how to address future situations more constructively as a consequence of the author's poignant insight. Indeed, this work is as promised, 'an enlightened approach to accelerated productivity.'"

FREDERICK FRANK
VICE CHAIRMAN, LEHMAN BROTHERS

"Ms. Anderson identifies and solves perhaps the most frustrating business problems — achieving changes, dealing with executive resistance, overcoming bullying, building successful meeting dynamics — by sharing an amazingly intuitive change process."

ROBERT SABATH
DIRECTOR, DELOITTE & TOUCHE

"Anderson's words and anecdotes speak volumes – her engaging style makes this a practical read that you will refer to again and again. Anything is possible!"

DR. BRUCE COOPER
VICE PRESIDENT, AVENTIS, INC.

"The process of learning about barriers and weaknesses through our experiences with others and then, through introspection, learning to modify our own behavior, is truly an 'enlightened approach to higher productivity.' I found myself totally engrossed in the book!"

L. MERILL BRYAN, JR.
SENIOR VICE PRESIDENT AND CIO, UNION PACIFIC CORPORATION

"Judith's book brings forth a whole new perspective on how understanding human relationships and behaviors in organizations is the key to productivity."

PATRICK LEPORE
PRESIDENT, CARDINAL HEALTHCARE MARKETING SERVICES

"Anderson's teachings and insights have released passion within our company. We have stopped a lot of our unproductive "blaming" behavior . . . now we go for the learning. What she articulates in the book is possible."

MARIE ADLER-KRAVECAS
PRESIDENT, MYRON CORPORATION

"This remarkable book addresses the next frontier of corporate improvement in a highly unique and effective way. Unquestionably, it is a tremendous tool for any corporate manager."

BARCLAY HOPE
PRESIDENT, ALBERT'S ORGANICS

"A must read for managers looking for increased productivity and improved working environments by building effective relationships."

SWROOP SAHOTA
VICE PRESIDENT QUALITY OPERATIONS, SCHERING-PLOUGH

"This is a must read for CEOs who wonder why their organizations are not more productive."

C. BARRY SCHAEFER
MANAGING DIRECTOR, THE BRIDGEFORD GROUP

"Judith Anderson demonstrates the unique ability to cut to the chase with corporate management and get away with it."

CLIFFORD F. LYNCH
PRESIDENT, C.F. LYNCH & ASSOCIATES

"The Path to Corporate Nirvana is exceptionally rich. My only regret is that this book was not available twenty years ago."

ROBERT V. DELANEY
VICE PRESIDENT, CASS/PROLOGIS

"The path of self-discovery shows that even the most cynical of us can learn to face ourselves as being the greatest barrier to increasing the effectiveness of our organizations."

RICHARD SHORTEN
CHAIRMAN, TEC INTERNATIONAL

"The author's personal reflections provide a unique perspective on the challenging dynamics of the workplace. Her pathway of learnings serves as a powerful guide for the reader to optimize performance and results."

"Judith Anderson's modest and reverential writing style makes for easy reading, which, to a casual reader, might belie the wisdom and depth of the theories and methods she so credibly describes."

The Path to

CORPORATE
NIRVANA

The Path to

CORPORATE NIRVANA

*An Enlightened Approach
to Accelerated Productivity*

JUDITH ANDERSON

Salem, Oregon

The Path to CORPORATE NIRVANA
An Enlightened Approach to Accelerated Productivity

Silver Falls Press
1680 95th Avenue NE
Salem, OR 97301
T 503-375-7750
F 503-375-7650
www.SilverFallsPress.com
info@SilverFallsPress.com

ISBN 0-9724041-0-4 / $24.95
Library of Congress Control Number: 2002111962

Publisher's Catloging-in-Publication
(Provided by Quality Books, Inc.)

Anderson, Judith, 1951-
   The path to corporate nirvana: an enlightened
approach to accelerated productivity / Judith Anderson.
   p. cm.
   LCCN 2002111962
   ISBN 0-9724041-0-4

   1. Industrial productivity.   I. Title.

HD56.A53 2003   658
                        QBI02-200745

Illustrations by Lauren Ottersten

Cover Photo: Douglas Reid Fogelson
Cover Design: Shelley Noble
Interior Design: Dotti Albertine
Judith Anderson Photo: Peter Dressel

DEDICATION

This book is dedicated
to all those who set an intention
each day to grow and learn.
And to Robert, who has been willing
to grow and learn beside me.
Bless you!

ILLUSTRATIONS BY
LAUREN OTTERSTEN

CONTENTS

FOREWORD

I will gain more understanding when I realize spiritual malnutrition is a condition that can be cured.
— IYANLA VANZANT

This book is based upon my experiences working with a large number of corporations as a consultant, and prior to that, working for several organizations as an employee. I have taken care to change the responses of my clients and associates to protect their anonymity; it needs to be stated that the individuals and companies reflected in these stories do not refer to specific individuals or organizations.

With regard to my own part—my thoughts and feelings as these circumstances unfolded—I have done my best to honestly portray my own learning process. This has not always been comfortable. In many situations while writing this, I saw a desire on my part to present myself in a more appealing way. However, it has been valuable to me to become aware of this, and to learn from it.

Individuals who experienced these events with me would likely have different memories and certainly different perceptions and interpretations of these experiences. All of that is fine, and as it should be. We see what we see because of what our experiences have been up to that point.

I have had a constant guide throughout the process of writing this book and it has been a rewarding experience. At the time of initiating this project, I was working full time, a parent, wife and friend, and engaged in the final year of a Masters Degree program in Spiritual Psychology at the University of Santa Monica. One of the many assignments we were given in the graduate program was to take on a project, something significant, something that would change our lives and the lives of others. I chose to write a book.

Early in this endeavor, I realized that I would not be able to write the way I typically write—which was at that time to brainstorm my ideas, develop an outline, prepare a rough draft, redraft, cut and paste, and so forth—in other words, an "intellectual" approach. I just didn't have the time. But the purpose of the school project was to take us outside our comfortable way of working—to challenge it and to develop new strategies for success. We were told we would need to invent new ways of working in order to handle the workload of the program.

I had been working with "dream states" at the time—posing challenges at bedtime, asking the "creative consciousness beyond," my term for accessing Spirit for creative insight, to guide me in my dream state toward the answer to a dilemma or question, and if it was for the "highest good of all concerned," that I awake with the solution in a way that I could understand it.

When I presented the challenge of how to write this book at bedtime, what I received the next day was, "just write." And so I began, with no thought of achieving more than a free-form stream-of-consciousness. I wasn't concerned with whether this would help me reach my goal, I was trusting the process.

Slowly in the weeks that followed I began to see that what I was doing was constructing a series of vignettes, each with a common theme.

I began to get more specific with my bedtime intentions: "What is the title of the first chapter and how does it begin?" Each time I did this, I would awake seeing pictures and words on paper. And that is what I wrote for a few hours each morning. At times, I would have the sense that I hadn't yet learned what I needed to learn to end a chapter—to resolve a situation about which I had been learning, for example, the topic of betrayal. In those situations, I would ask to be given an experience that would assist me in learning what I hadn't yet learned, and these experiences would seem to appear shortly thereafter. As the writing experience unfolded, the connection strengthened between what happened in my life and what I most needed to learn to complete this project. My gratitude for this process of learning deepened.

As a result, I offer this book as a "co-creation with Spirit." This collaborative, creative experience has been more rewarding than anything I could have dreamed up on my own.

Along the way, I have also had earthy, practical assistance which has had its rewards as well. First, my business colleagues Jim Rust, Tom Dyer, and Jennifer Dolan, and new associate Peggy Nagae, who traveled through many of these experiences with me and assisted me with my learning process, and especially my partner Tom whose insights, understanding and astute observations of personal dynamics have been so helpful to me. Because of the gift of collaboration which I experience with him, Tom has been instrumental in my learning how to work with individuals and organizations to realize the value of a collaborative path.

I am indebted to my clients who have entrusted me with their challenges and dilemmas, spoken openly with me about them, and trusted me to support them toward their goals. Their talents, creativity, energy, passion, intellect, insight and humor inspire me to learn more. My commitment to provide ever more meaningful service to them inspires me to keep learning.

I am also grateful to Michael Hagen whose many illustrations early on in the project helped me believe that the book was possible, and whose creative talent left me smiling and delighted on many occasions.

I want to thank Lauren Ottersten who took some of Michael's ideas and some of my ideas and added many of her own to help bring humor and art to these pages. Lauren's interpretations of the words help me see the chapters in new and useful ways. Thank you Lauren!

My gratitude also extends to my editor, Arthur Boehm, who has survived countless editing rounds in preparing these vignettes for publication. His patience and skill are bountiful. And to publicist Yvette Cohen-Pomerantz and agent Carol Mann whose early encouragement and conceptual input were helpful.

I would like to extend my appreciation to everyone at Silver Falls Press and Smarketing who assisted me in bringing this book to fruition: Ellen Reid, Laren Bright, Dotti Albertine, Shelley Noble, Lynne Bailey and Barbara Klui. Also, Karen Schalhoub and Susan Furey-Lloyd, whose interjections of talent and enthusiasm toward the end of this project were much appreciated, and especially Jeanie Lehman who has supported me faithfully, and with such competence, for so many years.

I also want to thank my USM classmates, the staff of USM, the MSIA and Insight organizations, the Ladies of the Club, the First Friday Group, and Philomena Casey, for their active support of the project, and caring, for which I am so grateful.

Finally, I would like to acknowledge my husband Robert, and our children Eric and Kira, my brothers Dick, Jim, Bob, Ron and Dan, and sister Jeanie; my mother Darline; my father Tony (in memory); the extended families of Bielenbergs, Wards, Staffords, and Andersons; and my dear friends over the years for supporting me on this journey. I love you all.

INTRODUCTION

Making the best of things is a damn poor way of dealing with them.
— ROSE WILDER LANE

Anyone who has ever worked in a corporation knows that nirvana is not the word to describe most of what happens during the day. Employees often withhold information and support from one another because to offer them might seemingly jeopardize a vested interest, a relationship, or what they perceive as their personal security. This is unpleasant to experience.

Individuals walk into meetings, their minds full of insights, information and creative ideas, but leave disengaged, sometimes "happy" simply to have their jobs, and feeling they are powerless—victims of a system that imposes "unfair rules" upon them. Individuals work hard, bring their talents to the table, solve complex challenges, identify exciting opportunities for their organization— and still end the work day feeling that what they offer isn't fully appreciated. They rehash the innuendoes, slights, and difficulties they've experienced again and again, hoping that with each replay the problem will resolve itself.

They develop coping strategies instead of learning strategies for addressing the challenges of corporate life.

> **An executive with a major corporation recently put the facts on the table to her company's CEO about why a major customer had been lost. The CEO responded, saying, "Well, one thing is for sure—I can always count on you to tell me the truth." But the executive told me she'll never speak directly like that again because she realized the CEO didn't want the truth; she could tell by his sarcastic tone and shake of his head that her openness was not really welcome.**

Experiences like this can "teach" us that our only option is blaming, complaining and putting up with the "reality" of life on the job. But the impact of this belief on ourselves and others is devastating to productivity, enthusiasm, creativity, innovation, and commitment. Real problems needing real attention do not surface as quickly as they could; innovative solutions are locked behind tight lips; and creative approaches die on the vine. Withheld communication translates directly into withheld passion, and productivity and creativity suffer. Our research indicates that a substantial loss in productivity results from withholding ideas and information that could make a positive difference in the jobs we are asked to do. In a global environment, with the pace of change accelerating, companies can no longer afford the luxury of a slow dance around critical issues.

But in spite of dozens of books on authentic communication techniques, truth-telling in the workplace, seminars on building open work environments where empowerment is the practice, individuals can often fail to experience meaningful change. "Blind spots" often prevent us from seeing how seminar and book materials relate to us; we only see how it relates to others. A good example showed up not long ago:

> **The vice president of human resources of a global transportation company called me to talk about spending a day with the management team. He wanted to build greater trust in his company so that decisions would be more collaborative and there would be less back-biting and sabotage. I knew the company well. "That sounds worthwhile," I said encouragingly, "but building open relationships is not a one-day event—it takes commitment to a sustained effort in order to change the behavior that creates distrust."**
>
> **"I know that," he said, "but we can't tell the president that just yet. He won't understand. I figure we'll start with the one-day program, and once that happens, we'll spring the rest of it on him."**

The vice president didn't see that he was engaged in the very behavior he wanted to change, a blind spot that would make it difficult for him to lead by example.

Emotions, if we know how to use them, guide us toward identifying and opening up blind spots just like

his. This insight comes as a shock to executives who operate out of the "old school" belief that emotions don't have
a place in the workplace. But if we don't recognize our
upset feelings—apathy, feeling misunderstood, fear, envy,
anger, resentment, pride and judgment—and handle them
effectively, the emotional upset shows up as unproductive
behaviors like stubbornness, pretending, complaining,
blaming others, pushing views, being righteous, being vin-
dictive, sarcasm, being territorial, being abrupt, withdraw-
ing, and acting "above it all".

In this unproductive mode, we are not developing or
leveraging the qualities and skills that will enable us to
address challenging situations. We are not using qualities
and skills such as flexibility, optimism, honesty, authentic-
ity, being OK with being wrong, being willing to support
others, offering views, staying engaged in passionate discussions, listening and acknowledging.

It takes sophisticated skills to shift from a blaming and
complaining mode, and unproductive behaviors, to a
learning mode and productive behaviors. This is particularly the case when you are trailblazing, creating change,
and others around you continue to operate from a traditional handbook. The path to corporate nirvana involves
developing new skills which accelerate productivity in
individuals and corporations, including the ability to use
them even while trailblazing. And emotional awareness is
the key that unlocks the access to these new skills. It is not
simply that emotion-based skills belong in the workplace,
it is that they are key to accelerating productivity.

Once these skills are internalized, the experience of
walking through the door to go to work is fundamentally

different. Instead of "bracing for the day," or sagging under the weight of what will "undoubtedly" take place, or longing for what could but won't happen, we experience light-heartedness, gratitude, enthusiasm and the expectation of success. The experience of corporate nirvana is one of walking through the work door to be with people that we care about, to do work that is important, and to express fully our passion, talent, creativity, and ideas—to be who we fully are.

Starting down the path to corporate nirvana requires that we take responsibility for our experiences. This means that instead of saying: "That is the way it is around here, and there is nothing that can be done about it," one asks, "What would I need to learn to handle even this situation with grace and ease?"

The most important skill needed to step onto the path to corporate nirvana is learning to tell the truth to oneself about what is going on. This requires self-trust for such truthfulness can cut to the very core of our being.

"Yer talkin' nirvana!" a client, Pete, exclaimed while we were talking about his company and his frustration that his peers often badmouthed one another in "one-to-one" discussions with each other. I had suggested that Pete speak to his peers about their behavior and how it was preventing them from coming together as a fully supportive, open and productive management team. "What you're saying would be great, I'll give you that, but what you're talking about is never going to happen. Some people are just

**going to be dishonest no matter what you do."
Pete was suggesting that heading in the direction
I suggested, speaking openly with his peers about
his wish that they not badmouth one another
was senseless, because nothing was ever going to
happen differently in his company. He might be
willing to change his behavior, he told me, but
others wouldn't change theirs.**

Being truthful inwardly requires taking the time to
fully understand the inner experience—thoughts and feelings—embedded in this type of exchange. I have found
the easiest way to teach others the skill of "revealing their
inner process" is to model it by revealing my own.

In the example above, my response was stunned
silence. I felt slighted that my idea had been summarily
dismissed. However, I barely took the time to notice that,
because in a flash I was internally dismissing Pete as "just
not getting it." When someone doesn't accept what I'm
saying, I can feel nervous, and I can question my ability. I
can have thoughts like 'Maybe I am talking nonsense.
Maybe I am not any good.'

But quickly, to cover up this fear—the concern
that I might not be perceived as good—I can make the
person I am speaking with "wrong" and dismiss them as
not being as "enlightened" as I am. And to cover up that
I'm dismissing them, I pretend otherwise, laughing off
their comment. In other words, I do the very thing
(behave in less than a fully honest way) for which I'm
making them wrong.

As I learn to correct my misinterpretations of reality

(for example, that my "goodness" depends on other people's reactions to what I say; that to be acceptable, others must accept what I say), as I let go of the fear that I am not "good" and instead ground myself in the reality that I am learning and I'm doing fine, I stay more present and connected to myself and others and more attuned to what is happening.

And as I continue on this learning path, I know that next time I will be able to see the meaning of Pete's pushback more clearly, sooner, rather than days later, as it happened this time. Rather than being absorbed by an inner drama, I will stay present and balanced and better able to recognize the information Pete is giving me about himself. Recognize, for example, that he will not head for a goal that he is uncertain of achieving. That his blind spot about badmouthing keeps him from seeing that he is engaging in the very behavior he doesn't like. That he uses the behavior of others, rather than his own principles, as a guide. And next time, I will be able to use my assets and skills to more effectively support him in achieving his goals.

The skill of "processing" oneself from upset to more productive action requires recognition of one's own emotional reactions for what they truly are—indications of areas where we have judged ourselves unworthy. Other people trigger those reactions which make us uncomfortable, so we want to make others wrong and blame them. Switching from this response to one of introspection is a powerful tool. It frees us to speak the truth in ways that others can hear and keeps our energy focused productively toward goals.

These skills are beginning to be learned and used to

transform work environments from places where fear is used to control behavior to places where trust and collaboration are the norm.

The payoffs are huge. Productivity increases because information is brought forward sooner, and there is less resistance and sabotage because there is less fear. Instead of feeling *against* those we work for and with, we are *for* them and the goals we share. We feel supported, encouraged, and free to learn; and our passion, creativity, and inventiveness spring forward naturally. People want to work in "learning-based" companies because all of their talents and contributions are wanted and utilized. Instead of "going to work" they have the experience of "going to the place where they do their life's work."

As I engage clients, what seems to hold them back most is the fear of revealing that they don't have the answers, that they are still learning. This is especially true as one goes up the organization, to more senior positions. Some individuals in upper management feel that others won't respect them if they reveal their vulnerabilities.

So I have come to see that my willingness to reveal my own vulnerabilities and emotional processes—and to show that doing so is not always easy or straightforward—has been especially helpful. This is particularly the case when I am able to do so in the moment, almost paradoxically, as I'm learning to do it. Showing this process in action is the purpose of the seven vignettes that follow; by unfolding my own quest for learning, I want to encourage others to initiate and deepen their own journey. In this way, individuals become their own best guide along the path to corporate nirvana.

➤ **The S-File** introduces Sam, a patriarchal CEO surrounded by employees who are fearful of telling
him the truth. Sam's patterns helped me learn
about the importance of self-trust and its value in
a collaborative environment.

➤ **Learning to love PNVs (Popping Neck Veins)** is
about anger in the workplace and how I learned to
uncover the fears my anger concealed. Anger
assisted me in seeing how I projected my deepest
fears onto others until I was strong enough to take
a clearer look at myself.

➤ **Et tu, Brute** is about betrayal in the workplace and
the importance of establishing big goals to create a
high-performing team. Acts of betrayals by others
revealed how I betrayed myself.

➤ **Balking Heads** looks at aligning authority and
responsibility in the work environment; how
resistance and defending hampers productivity.
These situations helped me see my resistance to
learning about how I resisted others.

➤ **Joining the AAA Club** shows how to use aggravation with others to reveal what is most needed to
handle aggravation at work. These lessons helped
me see how to reach goals with greater grace and
ease, and less trauma and drama.

➤ **A Hole in the Road** is about using repetitive failure patterns constructively to create successful
breakthroughs. When I learned to use what happens in the workplace to reveal what I needed to
learn about myself, I shifted from automatic pilot
in life to steering my own path to success.

➤ **Going, Going, GONG** taught me how to use the "gongs" in life, disappointments and disapproval by others, to develop the creativity and intuition that helped me find innovative solutions to key challenges.

The ability to use what actually happens in my encounters with others, to see their processes and reveal my own, and use this enlightenment to accelerate productivity in myself and others, has been my path to corporate nirvana. I have learned to see situations not as good or bad, but as data, as learning opportunities. By no means do I see the end of this journey—I am still fully in learning mode. The willingness to admit this, first to myself and then to others, has been amazingly helpful. When I reveal my learning process, it's not only supportive to others, but also accelerates my own learning. And learning in the corporate environment is, finally, what this book is about.

THE **S-File**

Truth
Telling
with
a
CEO
who
doesn't
want
to
hear
the
truth

▼

Wisdom
does not reside
in one head alone.

—

GHANAN PROVERB

THE **S-File**

SAM was the president of a company and my most important client. He was also highly intelligent, engaging, and, I would often note, a highly patriarchal executive. I saw him as patriarchal because he held much of the decision-making authority for a billion-dollar-plus organization and exerted control largely through fear of reprisal. This could mean being placed on the "road-to-nowhere" career track, or public encounters during which his intellectual capacity and market experience could quickly reduce a less formidable individual to silence.

Our company had been doing a wide variety of consulting work for Sam's company for several years, largely in areas of traditional management focus such as reducing costs, improving customer service, and identifying strategies that would improve growth and shareholder value. Increasingly, we had been working side-by-side with individuals and teams, coaching them on ways to meet their goals with greater effectiveness. We did this by identifying the roadblocks they encountered on the way to a goal. These roadblocks could indicate the need for systemic, structural or personnel changes, but more often were

Achilles' heel issues that limited the person or team *whenever* they pursued a goal.

Mostly we worked at the vice president and director levels, but on numerous occasions, I also worked with Sam. With whomever I was working, Sam's personality and command over the organization were significant parts of the equation.

Wherever I went in the organization, Sam's behavior was a source of wide speculation. Could anyone who had not demonstrated years of personal loyalty to him rise to the officer level? Did he purposely have his niece involved in projects (as a consultant) to have trusted eyes and ears in the room? Since he had millions, and seemed more engaged in defending against intruders than in building a company, why exactly was he working?

About two things, however, there was no debate: first, you don't go against Sam on anything and survive, and second, he's brilliant. The first time I met Sam, I was curious to collect my own impressions on both of these points.

I was leading a two-day discussion with his management team as a facilitator. My job was to moderate a discussion by standing at the front of the room with a flip chart and markers and keep the discussion on track— ideally to help create an environment in which everyone participated openly and honestly.

After that meeting, there was no doubt in my mind that Sam was an astute thinker who was often able to conclusively assess a matter while almost everyone else was still midstream in considering it. As to his reputed score-keeping, the evidence was murky; Sam seemed to appreciate an open and candid exchange of ideas—he encouraged it.

Still I had heard the rumors that Sam got personally involved in all promotions at the managerial level and above, and that if you made a particularly poor presentation, or "pissed him off" by behaving in a way that he didn't agree with, "your career was over." In one such case, a local-area sales manager had passed out squishy apples to help customers exercise their wrists. When Sam found out

There will be no dumb ideas around here.

that someone had done this without his authorization, the repercussions were such that for months after, all creative ideas had to meet the squishy-apple test: "Any concern here that we have another squishy-apple idea?" a manager might say, "because I don't need that write-up in my file!"

Concern about whether or not Sam would like an idea was all important—not whether or not an idea would further or hinder company goals. Naturally, a great deal of effort was involved in sending messages up through the chain of command to test ideas in advance, even with matters of little importance, just to minimize the chances of an employee finding himself at cross-purposes with Sam. All this took time. And there was enormous water-cooler energy invested in the process of looping through any questionable idea again and again. In the organization, anticipating Sam's reaction was known as "the S factor." And my observation of it became my S-File.

The number-one bone of contention in Sam's organization was the hours of work that were seemingly required to get the job done—long days, weekends, interrupted vacations. The consensus among those who worked for Sam was that if there were greater employee empowerment, the work could get done more effectively. Everything seemed to take more time than it should have because of "the S factor". While work/family-life balance and burnout were discussed at management meetings, there was little willingness to give Sam feedback about how his management style was involved in the problem.

I sometimes confronted the reluctance of employees to speak truthfully when I heard these complaints about Sam. I would sagely offer, *"A complaint is always about an unwillingness to speak the truth or to see the truth of a situation."* The recipient of this message would inevitably shake his or her head and say, "You're a consultant, you don't understand what it's like to work here. Sam would just as soon take you out; it's not worth the risk."

Privately, I'd shake my head at these comments, disappointed by the speaker's lack of willingness to address issues that needed attention. How did they expect the situation to change if they were unwilling to challenge the status quo? I cavalierly concluded that if I were in their shoes, I would charge into battle. In doing so, I assumed I could see the truth of the situation. But what I *didn't* see at the time was what my judging their unwillingness to learn how to give feedback was revealing about me.

Eventually, the turnover rate in Sam's organization raised the subject of morale high enough on the corporate radar screen for Sam to agree to undertake the company's first-ever employee attitude survey. In this process, which has become common in organizations, employees are asked to fill out an anonymous questionnaire in order to give feedback about how they experience the work environment and what changes would make it possible for them to be more effective. (With any survey of this nature, it can be better for management not to ask for employee input rather than to ask and then not respond to it, because asking for it sets up expectations that there will be positive change.)

Some time later, in preparation for an off-site team-building session I was to facilitate, a vice president shared the recently completed survey results with me. He had been concerned about the morale in his department, which he had recently taken over, and wanted to discern how much of the problem was created by the company at large and how much of it could be addressed through his willingness to make changes.

As my partner and I studied the responses to the survey, the broad results jumped off the page: employees did not trust management to lead them effectively. This was revealed in responses to questions that probed whether employees were clear about where the organization was heading. For example, 65 percent of the employees said that they did not believe senior management was aligned toward a common goal. This is akin to a group of people trying to pull a heavy sled up a hill without any agreement about the specific destination. More work will be done than is necessary. Individuals in Sam's organization worked hard but made little progress. The survey was revealing the dynamics behind this situation.

While the lack of alignment within senior management around common goals certainly matched our experience, the extensive negative commentary in the survey indicated that employees were clearly in a "blame and complain" mode and taking full advantage of having a safe vehicle for expressing their frustration. My partner and I have found in our consulting work that individuals who do not share a common goal tend to rally around common complaints. In this environment, there is little innovation. Anyone who sticks his neck out too far can quickly become the target of this rallying-around-blame game. This sets up an environment of playing it safe, where creativity and imagination are stifled. And when individual creativity is withheld, our passion has no fuel, no spark. So it is in the relative safety of complaining that our energy revs up.

The bottom line conclusion the survey revealed was a lack of confidence in leadership. A game of finger-pointing emerged in the interpretation of the source of this problem. Those who reported to Sam—the individuals one level below (such as the vice president of operations and the vice president of marketing)—interpreted the results as a lack of confidence in Sam. "See how it is?" one vice president said to me. "The organization has no confidence that Sam has a plan for where this company is going. And he plays us against each other. He asks two of us separately to solve the same problem, and it turns out to be twice as much work for everyone, in addition to undermining trust and collaboration."

Sam's interpretation of the survey results was that the problem lay with his direct reports: the group of vice presidents below him needed stronger leadership skills. Elsewhere in the organization, the problem was viewed as pertaining to "everyone above us."

> **A game of finger-pointing emerged in the interpretation of the source of this problem.**

The survey results, and more importantly the response of Sam's organization to the results, all fit the model of a traditional, patriarchal organization. In these organizations, characterized by a command-and-control style of holding decision-making authority at the top of an organization, the rush to blame is common. If something is wrong in the organization, then someone must be at fault. The usual response to a problem is: "Who made the mistake?" This sets up employee fear of exposure and shame on the one hand, and concern about how they will be disciplined for mistakes on the other. While tracking organizational problems to their cause can be quite helpful, the presumption in a patriarchal organization is that someone is to blame and should have known better, which instills fear. The underlying managerial tone becomes that of a parent delivering a reprimand.

Conversely, in what we call a collabo-

rative organization, the focus is on using all available information for learning about how to reach goals ever more gracefully and easily. In this kind of organization, if something is not working, the idea is to gather around, figure out what is going on, and decide how to fix the problem. The underlying presumption is that, since all employees are connected, probably everyone has a role in making the needed adjustments—even top management.

This shift in orientation, from blaming to learning, is key to accelerating productivity. In an environment where there is no trust, where people are likely to be blamed and called on the carpet for screwing up, critical information will not flow freely. Information about what needs to be changed in order to meet goals more effectively will not be offered. In the new millennium, with the pace of change continuing to speed up, delays created by withheld information or support are becoming too costly.

So as we reviewed the survey results, and matched it against our general understanding of patriarchal organizations, we reflected on how the distrust of leadership showed up as distrust in general in Sam's organization. There were many indications of how this adversely affected productivity.

For example, in Sam's company, the further up the organizational chain you went, the worse commitment-keeping got, even with regard to simple commitments, such as the time a meeting would start. (Even minor commitments like this affect the general atmosphere of trust: if I don't trust you to show up on time, why should I trust you to do what you'll say you're going to do?) This set up an insidious belief structure that the more responsibility you had, the less people could count on you to keep your word. Not keeping commitments to others, especially about time, became a way of demonstrating that you had Sam's ear.

> **When people are blamed for screwing up, information will not flow freely.**

One meeting I attended with three of Sam's vice presidents, a so-called crucial meeting to resolve a dispute between them, was like musical chairs with the three popping up intermittently to run out to take calls from Sam, or to make calls while waiting for another to return. "Sorry, but Sam really needed to speak to me," (ergo: I'm important) was said again and again that day. It didn't take much analysis to determine their level of commitment to resolving the dispute. What was clearly more important than working effectively together was responding to Sam.

At the time, I saw these patterns, saw how they related to the survey results, and to basic issues of trust, and I saw how I had been choosing not to bring the issues forward in a direct way. I began to see how by withholding this communication, I had become part of the broader "withholding pattern" in Sam's organization. I was withholding because that strategy seemed safest. My own issue of trust had become intertwined with the broad trust issues that were operating.

I brought this awareness with me into the meeting where I first reviewed the results of the employee attitude survey. The vice president had gathered sixteen directors out of town, away from the office, to set goals about what they wanted to accomplish together. Except they weren't together. When it came time to begin the meeting, a number of individuals were out of the room making phone calls. As they straggled in, others would dash out to engage in activities more important from their individual point of view. Clearly, I thought to myself, this group of directors is preparing for "vice presidentship" in this organization where being out of the room during a meeting is a status symbol.

It's an interesting dynamic that I've witnessed when facilitating meetings of this type: there is a goal, and then there is the way the group goes after the goal. In watching how the group behaves, what is revealed are generalized patterns that limit the group's effectiveness in going after any goal they have. Barriers are indicated when there is struggling, or a sense that we are not making progress—in this case the difficulty getting the meeting going after a break. This pattern revealed a lack of commitment to the group (as in, "My individual needs are more important than the group and the group's needs."). This lack of commitment was the more generalized barrier limiting this group's effectiveness. How a group responds when a barrier shows up (by ignoring it to avoid conflict, by blaming someone else for it, or by learning what it means) indicates how easily they will reach their goal. Because "blind spots" (i.e. patterns that limit our effectiveness but that we aren't willing to admit are there) operate with groups, as they do with individuals, groups sometimes can't see the barrier that is holding them back.

So I took a breath, saw that I had an opportunity to address the issue directly and asked individuals to share their experiences about how it felt to be overworked and kept waiting. As I did this, I could feel the palpable concern in the room—was it okay to speak this openly? And then all the pent up frustration they had been feeling came forward in waves. People talked about how when this happened, they pretended it didn't matter, that waiting on others was normal, but how on the inside they felt anger, irritation, and disappointment.

This is good, I thought to myself. We are building trust. The issues embedded in the attitude survey are being expressed, but in a way in which they can begin to be addressed: this group can decide that for the next three days, their meeting will start on time.

The willingness of the group to be aware of and discuss their feelings also opened the door to a discussion of the real issue: the lack of commitment to the group. They began to understand that starting on time was a metaphor for keeping commitments to one another generally and that keeping agreements builds trust. When the group saw that consciously choosing to keep agreements about time was a demonstration of support for one another—and they experienced the gratifying feeling of commitment to one another—their effectiveness in solving problems together increased exponentially.

Later, I reflected on what had happened. I had made it safe for myself to speak openly by telling myself that I don't have to know how to handle this situation, that I was there to support them and I was learning. This made it feel safe for me to ask about their feelings about commitment and trust and being kept waiting. When I had made it safe inside myself to be learning, it had seemed to make the room safe for others to learn. This "permission to learn" has been wonderfully freeing, and it seems that there is a fundamental link between giving oneself permission to learn and creating trust among colleagues.

Months passed. During this time, I was considering what next step made sense in terms of raising the issues of trust and commitment with Sam. Then, serendipitously, I found myself participating in a strategic brainstorming session with Sam and others about how the company might respond to a merger between two key suppliers. It was an interesting meeting because a number of outside educators who had been tracking industry developments had been invited to attend along with top executives in Sam's company. The CEO of the parent company was there as well. It was the one time I was in a meeting with Sam during which he had little to say. I interpreted this as a desire to avoid revealing any differences with his boss's positions and I wondered whether such disagreement would be of more concern to him or to his boss.

I spoke to Sam on one of the coffee breaks. "You know," I said, "I've been doing quite a bit of work with your organization in different departments. If you'd be interested, I would sure like to sit down with you and share some general impressions of what's going on with the culture here. Some of this may be relevant to the results of the attitude survey. Would that be of interest?"

"I would bet that's true," Sam said. "You may know quite a bit about what is going on around here. Consultants have that advantage. You talk to one group, then another, then another, and then you put the pieces together about how it all interrelates." Sam asked me to make an appointment with his office. I was left wondering if Sam really thought it was so great that an outside consultant knew so much about what was going on in his company.

I got nervous. Was he going to be able to hear my feedback? Would I be able to deliver it effectively? Would he shoot the messenger? Would my trip to his office be my last walk down the hall in this company? Sure, I felt the pain in the organization and knew that if there was going to be change, then Sam would need to change. Wouldn't it be easier for an outsider to approach him with this message? Or was I biting off more than I could chew? I mulled and considered and in doing so, I momentarily disconnected from trust and the willingness to just be learning. However, I did not see this at the time.

Instead, seeking safety in numbers, I took the head of human resources aside, showed him our analysis of the results of the attitude survey, explained the plan to meet with Sam, and asked him if he wanted to participate. His eyes lit up and he sat forward, animated.

"This is *just* the kind of information we need to have surface," he said. "I've noticed these patterns in the com-

pany long before I took the human resources job. But you
know Sam. It's hard to get some of this up and on the table
with him. This could be just what we need to get the ball
rolling and start addressing the real issues around here."

Talking points in hand, my partner and I and the head
of human resources walked into Sam's office for the meeting and sat down. (We were starting the meeting 45 minutes late, but well within the company's internal standard
of acceptable wait time!) It became quickly apparent that
of greatest concern to Sam was any specif-
ic information we could provide on who
was saying what, or whether people were
slacking off. I was stunned by the degree to
which his questions underscored the very
issue of distrust that the employee attitude
survey had revealed.

> **If someone has information for you that they believe will help the company but they suspect you won't like it, do you think they'll tell you anyway?**

"Do you think people are really working here?" he asked. "What is your sense as
you walk around? Do people really have a
commitment to their jobs or are they just
showing up? Sometimes I wonder," he
mused. "It just doesn't seem like we have
the same work ethic around here as when
I was coming up the ladder."

The disparity between the questions Sam asked, and
his employees' experience of overwork and caring for the
company's success that I found throughout his organization, was startling. How could it be that Sam's experience
and that of his staff were so different?

"Do you think you are getting open, honest feedback
from your people?" I asked curiously, seeing how that

could be one explanation for how Sam's perspective and his staff's perspective could be so different.

Sam answered, "You've been in some of our meetings—you see the way the debate goes. I think people are saying what they think."

"Yes," I agreed, "those discussions are free-flowing. But what I'm asking is: if someone has information for you that they believe will help the company but they suspect you won't like it, do you think they'll tell you anyway?"

Sam stopped breathing long enough for me to know that the question had been heard. I could see the implications of my question gathering in his quick mind, and then he turned to the head of human resources with a questioning glance. This is it, I thought to myself. The door is open. Here we go.

But the head of human resources shrugged his shoulders, shook his head, and said, "I always think I can say what I really think to you, Sam." I heard the door close. He had said what he thought Sam wanted to hear, letting Sam off the hook; he withheld what could have been powerful feedback. The head of human resources was still sitting on the couch, but he wasn't in the room.

This is classic, I thought to myself. It's not safe right here, right now for the vice president of human resources to speak honestly, and once again Sam is getting a distorted picture of the world he is intimately involved in creating.

I tried again, speaking of commitments and truthfulness, the relationship between behavior and trust, and between trust, creativity, and passion. But I had lost Sam. I could see he felt that what I was saying didn't have anything to do with what was going on in his company.

I tried data. "People know when they are being asked to buy an official stance that differs from their experience," I said. "And that undermines trust. For example, look at the way the results of the attitude survey are summarized. The straight way to talk about the results on leadership would be: 'Fifty percent of the employees indicated they receive less than half of the direction they would like.' But look how the report summary presents that: ' . . . eighty-eight percent of employees give ratings which are distributed from one to seven across the satisfaction scale, resulting in an index of 0.92 for this key area.'"

I glanced at my partner who had so quickly seen the real impact of the data, seen how the report's presentation had clouded it, and was now wondering if the truth was going to be heard.

Sam said, "I agree that the vice presidents could use some development—they're not as strong in the area of leadership as they could be. But frankly, I think we're addressing that. Actually, I don't think your information is all that current. A lot of this is being addressed with programs we recently launched. I think you're going to see a big turnaround in the results of our next survey." I hesitated, wondering if I should agree with Sam's "wait and see" approach.

But I continued, still wanting to get through to Sam. I mentioned that his willingness to examine his behavior would make it safe for everyone else, particularly the vice presidents, to look at their own behavior. There were perhaps one or two moments when I imagined that the feedback had landed home, but I recognized that I had stopped short of a directness that I thought might jeopardize my standing with the organization. It wasn't worth risking the business relationship, I had decided.

The experience of delivering feedback into the blind spot of a successful executive is a challenge. The more successful an individual is, and the more he or she has job

performance tied to self-worth, the more difficult it can be for the person to consider how they can be more effective. I wince as I remember attempts by others to deliver feedback to the areas of my blind spots.

And I now understood more fully the difficulty of presenting Sam with information out of sync with his view.

I left Sam full of evidence about how his unwillingness to hear feedback was intricately related to the ineffectiveness of the organization. For a moment, just as I was leaving his office, I couldn't wait to find someone to share this with, someone who would agree with my view, my conclusions.

Then I stopped myself. I realized that I wanted to do exactly what I had judged others wrong for doing. I wanted to complain, just like employees who were stuck in complaining about Sam. I reminded myself of what I had said over and over, "Complaints are about an unwillingness to speak the truth or to see the truth of a situation."

When we complain, we distract ourselves from what we are feeling in the moment, emotions such as disappointment, frustration, anger, fear, or a sense of unworthiness. We soothe ourselves by finding people to agree with us that we're in the right and someone else is in the wrong. We feel better. This is what complaining accomplishes.

Underneath all this is a belief that what we need to do with negative feelings is soothe them away. Better yet, don't have them to begin with. Uncomfortable feelings are definitely to be avoided. We don't want to go there.

> **When we complain, we distract ourselves from what we are feeling in the moment.**

In complaining, we disregard our feelings—we make the issue about someone else or something else rather than about what is going on inside of us. This is a form of disrespect for our experience, for ourselves. Over time, this disrespect becomes distrust—not of others, as it might be comfortable to conclude, but of ourselves. We don't trust ourselves to know the internal experience we are having. And we miss the opportunity to learn based upon what emotion is surfacing in us. Conscious exploration of our inner experience, which often involves revealing a blind spot, gives us productivity-enhancing insights that are not available when we are operating on automatic pilot. We learn more about ourselves and can become more effective and productive.

When we get honest about
our internal experience . . .

> "I didn't feel safe speaking up fully before; now I'm judging that I could have done better."

And acknowledge this . . .

> "And that is just what happened. Sometimes I withdraw when I don't feel safe and then I judge myself for that."

And then are willing to assume that our experience just as it was is the ideal perspective from which to see what needs to be learned . . .

> "Maybe my instincts are correct, maybe speaking up at that time was not an appropriate risk. How is it that I am not fully trusting my instincts here? What is that about?"

And become willing to explore . . .

> "If I did trust myself fully, what is it that I would be willing to see about myself?"

And tap into inner wisdom . . .

> "I see that I can learn to trust myself more and respect my decisions in the moment. And I see I have more to learn about delivering feedback to CEOs."

By respecting our feelings, we make it safe to have our own internal experience. Regardless of what is happening externally, we experience greater inner safety if we validate our feelings than if we disregard or deny them. We can then view the world as a safe place because we are safe internally in the experience we are having. We begin to trust ourselves and the validity of our experience and what it has to teach us. We don't need to get rid of uncomfortable feelings, dissipate them through complaining or numbing-out. Instead, they become our road markers. We no longer become involved with something we may have done wrong. We can acknowledge with compassion that we are just learning, which has always been so, whether we've had the awareness to see it or not.

From this exercise, I could see that I had wanted to believe I knew how to deliver feedback to Sam. I recognized that my blind spot was in pretending I knew how to do this. That blind spot made it easy for me to dismiss the concerns of others who were also struggling with the problem. I had been cavalier in my response to them, and toward myself. The truth was, I was simply learning.

My need to complain about Sam faded. And as it did, I experienced a deepening gratitude for my willingness to learn and for life itself as a rich experience of learning.

About a year and a half went by after the feedback encounter with Sam. Our work with individuals and teams in the organization continued. The departure of executives at Sam's company seemed to accelerate, and many more talked about leaving. One morning, a vice president, Sam's protégé, had a cup of coffee with me.

"I don't know how much longer I can take it here," he said. "I mean, who wants to hang around when your ideas aren't listened to, your decisions are reversed, and you're not able to really contribute what you have to offer?" I was stunned. It must be bad if a person who had Sam's ear was so frustrated. How long could this really go on?

Several weeks later, the protégé left the company. Sam sent out an announcement about the departure over the company's internal phone broadcast system whereby a voice message could be left in the voice mailbox of every employee. As a tag to the announcement, he said " . . . and if any of you have some ideas about what we need to do differently around here, feel free to let me know your thoughts." This request for feedback certainly gave new meaning to the phrase "too little, too late."

Sam was fired two days later and escorted off the property. Unwilling or unable to give feedback, the company had made a last-resort decision and sent the message "this isn't working" in the only way it perceived it could.

A brilliant man, Sam was nonetheless his own worst enemy. Under him, his company was not able to be sufficiently responsive to the changes that the marketplace demanded, due in part to the ongoing turnover of employees and to the time spent managing "the S factor". Sam was smart enough to address the real problems, if he had known about them. But information about what issues needed to be addressed couldn't find their way to Sam's ears. Sam's blind spot was his inability to receive any course-corrective feedback that implied on any level that he could be more effective, and that his own ineffectiveness cascaded down to become the ineffectiveness of others. His success and track record gave him all the evidence he needed to dismiss those "underneath him" hierarchically and intellectually. He discounted those who might attempt to raise points that were uncomfortable for him. The information he most needed to hear couldn't reach him.

I thought about my meeting with Sam many times. How could I have been more effective so that more of the message I had for him could have been heard? What would it have been like to have had the skill to deliver feedback into his most protected blind spots—to build a level of trust with him that would have made that possible? And if building trust with others is a reflection of an opportunity to deepen self-trust, what was I still missing about myself?

Awareness seeped in slowly. Inviting awareness in an area in which we have confusion is perhaps the first step to greater awareness. I began to see that effectiveness has something to do with detachment from outcome because to the receiver of the feedback, the sender's attachment to sending it may feel like an attack (which, of course, could be accurate).

In other words, if my self-esteem is attached to Sam getting my message, then I will attempt to exert some influence along with my communication. Thoughts like, "What is the matter with you? Why can't you get this? You've got to get this point!" will underlie what I am saying. And the emotions behind those thoughts are what people may resist, intentions that have to do with my self-esteem concerns, which are themselves about fear and dis-trust. Of self.

I got it.

Why should Sam trust me? I was making my self-interest, my wanting to shore-up my self-esteem, my wish to feel safe, more important than creating a safe relation-ship with him.

Feedback doesn't necessarily happen verbally. Sometimes it takes the form of realizing that we've had a particular experience, or one similar to it, again and again. I was suddenly amused at my frustration with Sam's unwillingness to hear feedback when all the while there was feedback available to me which I had missed. When you can't hear, you don't.

Not long after this, I once again found myself with an opportunity to deliver feedback to a highly patriarchal president about the level of collaboration in his organiza-tion. As the time to do this approached, I was nervous but not enough to take anyone with me (like the head of human resources). I can do this, I told myself—it is only about learning. I noticed my fear, and in this awareness, much of it lifted. Greater self-trust inwardly was showing up as greater self-trust outwardly.

The feedback I had for the president was based on a benchmarking tool we had developed in our consulting practice called C-PAT, which stands for Collaborative-to-Patriarchal Assessment Tool. I had asked the president a series of questions designed to reveal what he believed about customers, vendors, mistakes, goals, and feedback. Based on his responses, we were able to systematically assess the level of collaboration in his organization—to discern the degree to which individuals worked effectively together, leveraging strengths to achieve passionately held shared goals. This report was based not so much on the content of what was said, but on our way of using responses to the questionnaire to reveal the underlying beliefs of the CEO. The survey also enabled us to identify what was blocking collaboration, and what specifically would have to change for additional collaboration to show up.

Through this work we had been learning just how a CEO's blind spot relates to the structural weaknesses of his or her organization. Over time, the organization unconsciously puts in place structures and processes to protect the CEO's area of sensitivity.

For example, presidents who place high expectations on themselves to be mistake-free will drive hard toward perfectionism. They may be quite good at building organizations that have excellent processes for producing systematic responses to routine situations—a real strength— but their success may be limited by their need to create "perfect" environments. In such situations, a CEO's belief that mistakes ought not to happen will influence all employees. The message employees get is ambiguous; a CEO may say, "It's okay to make mistakes around here as long as you learn never to make the same mistake again." Such statements, however, only create anxiety. Telling someone not to make a mistake twice is about as helpful as telling them not to make it once.

Someone who is rigidly mistake-averse will tend to make sure they find out who made the error and keep track to ensure that the same person doesn't make it again. Not exactly a safe environment in which to bring forward issues to benefit everyone's learning. If it's two strikes and you're out, then I would just as soon keep the first strike to myself, thank you very much.

Presidents who don't like to make mistakes will un-

"..thwarting the flow of information.."

consciously and understandably protect themselves from learning about one, and not much feedback will take place.

The inability to give a president feedback about how his or her behavior doesn't work gets institutionalized and is communicated in many formal and informal ways. For example, the president may demand that feedback be objectively accurate. If the person giving the feedback is upset, he or she may be told that the upset is evidence that the issue is with him or her and is not a company problem. Again, the free flow of information is thwarted. In such companies, there is generally no system to facilitate feedback from the bottom up on a routine basis. The pattern of no feedback locks in systematically as part of "the way things happen around here."

This is a patriarchal system disguised as a learning

organization. Management may say it wants to learn, but it tracks mistakes and mistake makers. The staff does its best and, at the same time, remains protective of information that might suggest it is doing less than the best possible job. Information about success surfaces more freely than does information about repetitive difficulties and ideas on how to alleviate them. Typically, no one mentions how it feels when they are under siege—or how unproductive they are during those times.

> **Presidents who don't like to make mistakes will unconsciously and understandably protect themselves from learning about one.**

So here I am, delivering feedback to this president about the C-PAT query and the level of collaboration in his organization. As I do so, I am aware that once again I am dealing with an intelligent, personable, and successful individual with a big blind spot about whether it is okay to be still learning. I make it okay with myself that I am just learning how to do this by silently telling myself 'It's okay, I don't have to do this perfectly, I am just learning here, I will just do my best, and what happens will just be what happens. No matter what unfolds, I will learn something valuable.' That eases things quite a bit inside me—I don't create an expectation that I must know how to do something, when the fact is I am still discovering how.

It's a difficult session. Whatever information I bring forward—for example, that his staff's reluctance to give the president feedback has something to do with how he receives it—is pounced on. "How can you say that?" or "That doesn't match with my experience around here at all" is his response, and I am provided with lots of stories and explanations. "People don't give me feedback because they are afraid that I will take it personally and not like them," he says. "No matter how many times I tell them to speak the truth, they just can't get past their fear to do it." I see the defense happen before the information I am offering is fully taken in and considered.

And then I just let go. I've been here before. I know how hard it can be to hear information about certain aspects of myself that I don't want to recognize. I realize it is not my job to convince this person of anything. I am here because I care about the organization and because I'm in service to this individual. I have feedback to offer. It may be on target, it may not be.

> The issue is, am I willing to express myself and offer my perspective even when that is difficult to do?

The accuracy of the feedback is not the issue. The issue is, am I willing to express myself and offer my perspective even when that is difficult to do? The issue is staying true to myself rather than pursuing approval through another's acceptance of my ideas. That is all. So in that brief moment of awareness, of seeing that I am attached to a certain outcome, I let go of it mattering that I'm heard.

And I say with neutrality because I am now neutral, "I am experiencing it as difficult to give you feedback." That's all I need to say because it says everything.

The president says, "Well, people tell me lots of things, you understand. I have to determine if it is accurate before I listen to it."

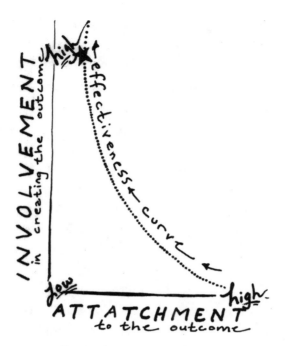

How come, I wonder? How come it's not safe to just listen? The goal of listening is to just listen, to hear what another person says, to hear out of respect for the person speaking. It doesn't matter whether we agree with the information being given. We can acknowledge people for caring enough to share their honest views and decide later if we agree with what is being said. Actually, if we are having any kind of resistance at all to what is being said, waiting is probably best. We have to see what our emotional reaction is about before we can fairly consider the accuracy of the information.

The commonly held misconception that attentive and respectful listening can only take place when we agree with what is being said, defies logic. How do we know what is being said unless we listen carefully? And once we've heard it, we need to test what we hear against what we have experienced. This can be done in a brief moment of pause and consideration before responding to what is said, and when this happens, the speaker has the sense that they are being heard.

My feelings have shifted. I don't need this person to validate me by understanding what I am saying. I can do that myself by listening carefully, by attuning to inner intuition, and by taking the conversation as an on-course/off-course validation of my perspectives. I stay in the learning mode, I stay out of the taking-it-personally mode—and, therefore, I stay effective.

I get honest with what my experience is in the moment and tell the president, "I'm pretty confident of our management assessment tool because we have used it many times with good results. I'm professional, and I have a good deal of experience dealing with senior management. And I am having trouble here expressing feedback such that I feel I am being heard. I am just wondering what it's like in this organization for someone without my level of experience and confidence to try to give you feedback."

I don't need him to get it; I don't even need him to hear me. I am here in service and support.

He says, suddenly much more open, "Well, your assessment of the environment here does not match my experience, but I am certainly willing to consider the possibility that my experience is not the experience of everyone. Why don't you survey my people? It can be anonymous. You can just send them a form and ask them to indicate on a scale of 1 to 10 how collaborative it feels around here. Who knows, you might learn something. I might learn something. We'll see. It will be interesting."

He has shifted, too. I sense it in the way he relaxes into his chair and starts to get curious about what the results might indicate. I suddenly see how dropping the attachment to being heard makes being heard more likely. And I get how being willing to learn, versus needing to already know, creates the sense of internal safety that makes dropping the attachment possible.

Weeks later, I talk with an employee with whom I'm friendly and who knew about my plan to meet with the president. "I don't know what happened between you two," she says, "but it's different here now. We're asked for input, and when we speak, we get listened to."

Obviously the president is a quick study.

I couldn't help thinking of Sam and the part he contributed to this meeting, to what I was learning. I appreciated that the experience of working with Sam had been one lesson along the way in my learning. I could see how exploring the encounter with Sam, and the issues of self-trust it surfaced, had made learning possible and increased my effectiveness in delivering feedback to this CEO.

But I also saw how I was still struggling to accept that my encounter with Sam was what it was, struggling to let go of the wish that it should have ended differently. The demand that I should have been able to do better with Sam—that I should have known more than I knew at the time—was a judgment, a demand that I be perfect. In seeing that I was still "threaded" to this perspective, I see how hard it can be to let go of the judgment at this level. This is helpful to see and unleashes more learning.

I am learning about surrender. I am learning about

> **My willingness to learn makes learning easier.**

trust. I am learning to accept that I am still learning. There is freedom in this awareness. My willingness to learn makes learning easier. While the path to learning is unpaved and unknown, it is the path I take.

Learning TO Love PNVs
(Popping Neck Veins)

What Anger and Other Strong Emotions Reveal in the Workplace

▼

Look at the word
responsibility –
'response-ability'
– the ability to choose
your response.

—

STEPHEN COVEY

CHAPTER 2

Learning TO Love PNVs

AT one point in my career, I found myself working for Matt, the senior financial officer of a major corporation. Our relationship was new, brought about by the recent and abrupt departure of my former boss and mentor.

The week after being given the news about my new reporting relationship, my new boss and I were to depart for a visit to a recently acquired company. I welcomed the opportunity to begin building what I hoped would be as good a relationship as I had had with my former boss. While on the surface there was nothing to be nervous about, I was anxious about how the initial getting-to-know period would go.

The morning of the trip I checked with Matt's secretary about how to coordinate the two-mile trip from the office to the hanger where the company jet was housed.

"Do you think he wants to drive so his car will be at the hanger when we get back?" I asked, "Or would he like me to drive us over?" My former boss and I had always driven together, so I assumed I would do so with Matt.

"I don't know," she said smiling, "I'll check and get back to you."

But she didn't.

About an hour later I happened to glance up and saw my new boss pushing the down-button near the elevator just outside my office door. Thinking I should join him, I grabbed my coat and briefcase, but before I could reach him, he had gone. "What's up?" I asked his secretary. "I don't know," she replied shaking her head, "I guess he forgot about you. You better just go to the airport yourself."

I managed to catch up with Matt on the other side of the hanger as he headed down the sidewalk to the company plane. The pilot and co-pilot were walking just up ahead of us, as were the controller and a junior analyst who were both traveling to the same destination as us, but on other business.

My boss turned and glared, his eyes drilling into me, his neck veins popping. "Look," he said through his teeth, "it's not *my* job to be chauffeuring you around! Your job is to be on the plane when it takes off. If you're not in your seat when it's time to leave, you don't go. How you get to the plane isn't my concern, but don't ever try that stunt again!"

Stunned, I walked the rest of the way to the plane a couple of steps behind him. So much for getting off to a good start I thought to myself with a heavy heart.

I meekly climbed aboard and sat down next to him in the only remaining seat available, wondering as I did whether there was some seat-assignment protocol that I should know.

Matt sat reading a newspaper, still smoldering throughout the takeoff. Mentally, I started updating my resume and reviewing my networking contacts. Maybe I

could call my just-departed boss and see what he was up
to...

Finally as the company jet began to level out, Matt
turned to me, now calmer, but still with a righteous attitude. "How did you and Larry handle traveling together?"
he asked about my former boss, apparently gathering evidence.

"Well," I said, struggling to anticipate what landmine
might lie ahead, "we'd always ride together. We'd decide in
advance which of us was driving—sometimes he did and
sometimes I did. If we weren't coming back together,
someone at the hanger would give the other person a ride
back to their car." It didn't seem complicated; what was I
missing?

Matt looked surprised, as if I had just said something
remarkable. After a pause, he said, "You have to understand, I often travel with the chairman, and the chairman
runs a tight ship. It's everyone's job to be on the plane
when the plane takes off and it's everyone's responsibility
to get to the plane on time. That's how it's done." He continued, increasingly caught up as he described the world of
senior management. "I've seen the chairman ask the pilot
to take off when someone was thirty seconds late," he said,
"and running from the hanger to catch the plane, just to
make a point. So you might as well know what goes on.
It'll be easier on you in the long run."

I thanked him for letting me know what was what,
and sat stone-faced for the rest of the trip, still smarting
from the embarrassment of a public dressing down. He
was not only behaving wrongly and inappropriately, I
thought—he was a jerk. I silently called him every offen-

sive name I could think of, but by the time the plane landed I had decided that maybe I was lucky to work for someone so intent, apparently, on teaching me the ropes. I
thought with his help I might quickly learn tips that
would help me ascend in the organization. Better, at least,
to be told the lay of the land than to try to operate without this information. Maybe I had been too shielded by
my former boss—maybe it was time to grow up and play
by the big boys' rules.

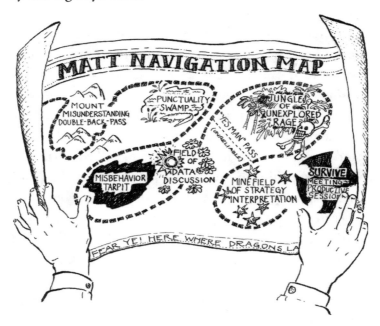

I did learn quickly—about avoidance and manipulation. I became quite sophisticated about how not to trigger Matt's anger, the pulsation of the blood vessels in his
neck, the rage that seemed primeval. Dealing with him
was indeed like stepping through a minefield; I learned
where I could and could not tread. Debating the interpre-

tation of data on the company's cost structure, for example, was fine. Challenging his thinking about the appropriateness of various marketing strategies employed by the divisions was not. Being proactive about what needed to be done and verifying priorities was good. Giving Matt feedback on the value of various meetings he asked me to attend was not.

> **I became quite sophisticated about how not to trigger Matt's anger, the pulsation of the blood vessels in his neck.**

I had to believe that others were caught in the same bind as I, guarding themselves against triggering his explosive rage. In departmental meetings, for example, controversial ideas were put forth tentatively then quickly withdrawn if Matt's jaw appeared to tighten even slightly. I began to imagine that elaborate under-the-table group strategies were operating; someone at staff meetings would invariably recount misbehavior having to do with a person outside our department just to discharge Matt's anger. We'd willingly sit through the time it took for him to vent because he wasn't angry with us and the rest of the meeting would go more smoothly.

Matt was good at what he did. As senior financial officer, he was an active and involved steward of the company's financial health. He always seemed five steps ahead of the curve. I admired his genius at seeing the pitfalls that lay just ahead, and at recognizing opportunities before anyone else did. He also carried substantial influence with the board of directors. There was speculation that he was a candidate for chairman when the current chairman retired. Putting up with his occasional PNV bursts seemed a small price to pay for the chance to work with someone as talented as he was.

Even so, I wanted him to change. What would it be like for me to operate with a higher level of integrity and not be "forced" to pretend or play games? What if I could just be honest?

Matt's problem with anger was keeping me from being effective. He needed to handle his problem.

Again and again I fantasized a pivotal life-altering conversation between Matt and me in which I would educate him about his anger so that he would immediately change his ways. He would be grateful to me, I could relax, and our department would move to a new level of effectiveness and camaraderie.

I was, after all, a student of anger. A couple of years earlier I had awakened to the effects of anger in a new way by connecting for the first time, consciously, specific physical sensations in my body with the emotion of anger. I had begun to recognize anger in myself that I'd never been aware of before and had even let loose a couple of times. I had read a lot about anger; I understood it. I could teach Matt how to deal with his rage.

"There's hurt underneath your anger," I would tell him. "You need to get at the hurt so you can heal it. Then you'd be a lot more effective because people wouldn't be so afraid to bring you bad news." I was put in his path to help him, I imagined. It was destiny.

The reverse—that he was there to teach me about myself, as he eventually did—didn't occur to me. His anger didn't seem to have anything to do with me; all I knew was that I suffered because of what he had yet to learn.

It didn't occur to me that he could teach me about myself because I wasn't yet safe enough inside myself to see the negative self-judgments I carried about anger and worthiness. My self-worth was dependent on others seeing the value of my contributions. When they did, I felt confident. When they didn't, I quietly and unconsciously seethed while playing it safe. At the time, my level of consciousness, the way I saw the world, led me to one conclusion: Matt's problem with anger was keeping *me* from being effective. He needed to handle *his* problem.

This may have been an accurate observation, but my reaction to his "anger problem" went way beyond evaluation —it involved strong negative judgment of him on my part. I condemned Matt for his bursts of anger, "made him bad" for not addressing it and—worst of all—made him wrong for not seeing that I could assist him in dealing with it.

What I didn't understand was that judgments like these offer a clue to our blind spots; when we make other people wrong it's evidence of strong negative judgments we hold about ourselves. Using our judgments of others to reveal our own self-judgments is a way to discover aspects of ourselves that would be helpful to see. My ability to use Matt as a mirror in this way—to reveal my own self-judgments about anger, holding back, and worthiness—was still embryonic.

The object in the mirror may be closer than it appears.

Most of us have been raised under a right-wrong model of the world. *These* behaviors are right, and people who act this way are good. But *those* behaviors are wrong, and people who do those things are bad. While consequences of behavior are important to learn, what we often learn instead is that unacceptable behavior makes us unacceptable as a person.

It's only a small leap to conclude that if throwing a tantrum means we're bad, then the feelings of anger that precede the tantrum are bad too. If we want to be good, to be worthy of recognition and love, to be accepted, to have security, then we had better not have bad feelings. Or, if we do have them, if we explode, then we need to quickly place blame on someone or something else that is the "real" problem—it's their fault that we feel angry, we tell ourselves. This dance of denial and projection is complicated to articulate, but it's something we learn to do in a right-wrong world before we learn much else.

The pattern of not seeing how we judge ourselves comes from fear, (we're afraid the judgment might be true), and we instinctively protect ourselves from this. It's automatic. On one level, it's wonderful that we can do this, that we can take care of ourselves in this way—that there is a sense of safety available to us that can keep us from seeing what is too painful to see until we are ready to see it. With more expanded consciousness, we recognize that there is only learning—that we can be safe in whatever experience we are having because we are just learning.

Once we have that insight, negative emotions (rather than being something to get rid of) become something of value. Emotions like anger, frustration, and apathy are windows through which we can exit the limitation of self-judgment. The more harshly we judge others wrong, the more emotion we have tied up in this response, the greater the amount of self-judgment. (Otherwise we'd just evaluate a situation with neutrality, rather than be emotional and judgmental about it.) So the judgments we make of others can assist us in seeing and then releasing self-judgment. Negative emotions are the gifts that reveal we have business to address with ourselves.

When we can use our emotional reactions to others as clues to how we judge ourselves, and when we learn how to let that judgment go, we open ourselves to the potential for exponentially greater effectiveness and productivity, because the drag of emotional negativity lifts.

When this awareness happens for the first time, it's often remembered as a pivotal moment. We see how all our experiences have been valuable for learning. We become able to consider the right-wrong model of the world as a choice with consequences. We are also free to choose a learning model—a model where experiences are neither good nor bad but opportunities to learn. The consequence of adopting a learning orientation is positive: learning accelerates.

This is not to imply that negative or limiting behaviors do not have adverse consequences, because of course they do. But our job is to de-link behaviors from feeling unconditional worthiness. When this de-linkage happens it becomes possible to consider our behaviors, not as evidence of goodness or badness but rather in terms of whether they work or not. We then act much as athletes who continuously improve their performance based upon microscopic experimentation with what works and what doesn't work. What works is what assists us in achieving our goals with greater grace and ease. What doesn't work is what limits us from achieving our goals, or makes them difficult to achieve. An approach free of negative self-judgment puts us on the path of learning and discovering. This moves us in the direction of nirvana, heaven on earth.

This skill—taking responsibility for our emotional responses and using them to eliminate self-judgments—is the next-frontier tool for enhancing business productivity. Using it is like using the moon's gravity to sling shot people into warp-speed, as in the movie *Armageddon*; it's possible to achieve a level of productivity or speed that simply wasn't possible before. Using our reactions to others as mirrors of our inner

world allows us to move toward our goals with greater
speed.

It's common to use others as role models when we see behavior that seems effective and we want to emulate it. Using our
negative reactions to others as a mirror of
ourselves is a similar but more sophisticated approach to revealing behavioral blind
spots and self-judgments. Doing so
requires new emotional skills, a willingness
to test the boundaries of what we are comfortable with knowing about ourselves,

> **The judgments we make of others can assist us in seeing and then releasing self-judgment.**

and the courage to face our fears. It requires redefining our
fears, our issues, and our challenges as blessings.

While a guide, teacher, friend or business colleague
may assist us in becoming clearer about all this, it is our
inner wisdom that must affirm the truth of it. When we
learn to honor this wisdom, our own sense of what is truly
happening becomes more important than the judgmental
messages we may receive from others. It may take a life-
time to access inner wisdom—it takes as long as it takes—
but once we do we possess the key to self-acceptance.

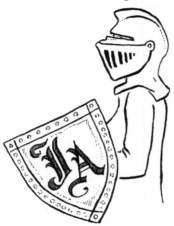

When we attune to
inner wisdom, we come to
know who we truly are and
how we are connected with
something greater. We see
that being who we are is not
dependent upon what we
do or achieve, but simply *is*.
Awareness that our worth

"just is" frees us from the need to demonstrate it, frees us from the fear that our worthiness can be stolen, lost or destroyed by an authority outside of us.

When I worked with Matt, however, I still felt that my worth as a person depended on my ability to achieve results. I was trapped in the right-wrong model and was never in a position to help Matt deal with his anger, as I had fantasized. And learning about myself wasn't as important to me as the task at hand: getting my own business started.

When I finally left the company, Matt said to me "I'm going to call you up one day, you know. I'll be running a company and I'll want you to head marketing. We'll be back together again one day, you'll see."

Maybe, I thought to myself, maybe. Could I ever feel safe with him? Could I ever trust him enough to be open? That seemed about as likely as actually having the conversation with him that I had rehearsed in my head so many times. His anger had always stood between us, and I couldn't see myself embracing an opportunity to encounter it in the future.

I spent the next four or five years establishing my own consulting business. Throughout this time it seemed as if my awareness of the emotional reactions in others was at the forefront of my experiences. I became more aware of the nature of my own feelings as well, but my ability to understand my emotional self was still rudimentary. Often I was aware of feeling generally upset, but wasn't able to more precisely name the feeling. But shifts in consciousness were underway. I began experimenting with observing my reactions to others as a clue to what I wasn't seeing about myself, often asking myself: 'What does my reaction to them show me about myself?' My skills were not yet honed. It can be difficult to accept the previously unacceptable before the antidote skill, self-forgiveness, has been learned.

My growing involvement in facilitating group discussions at that time was largely concerned with information and ideas. My skills at questioning, clarifying, and driving for results had found a productive outlet in facilitating brainstorming sessions that involved flushing-out the nuances of issues and developing plans and approaches to projects.

In doing this work, I was becoming increasingly aware of individual behaviors and attitudes that appeared to keep a group from achieving what it wanted to accomplish. I felt tentative about how much permission I had to address those issues directly in the groups with which I was working. Yet I kept returning to the question I had: How can I effectively raise and address these issues?

I set a clear intention to be open to learning about how to do this. Shortly after waving the wand of intentionality, I had the opportunity to have someone whose skills in facilitating group dynamics I greatly admired participate in one of my sessions. Her name was Marilyn. Just before the meeting convened I let Marilyn know that I was open to feedback from her about ways that I might improve my effectiveness.

The group consisted of human resource directors from a large manufacturing company. They wanted to discuss ways of restructuring their organization along processes as well as various ways of presenting traditional cost accounting data so the investment in specific processes would be revealed. The group had a new boss who was in the room, and I attributed the apparent "holding back" that soon characterized the discussions to that fact. Still, we made some progress.

In a debriefing after the meeting, Marilyn asked how I generally liked to receive feedback. I braced myself, thinking that I was in for criticism. There's only one way to receive it, I thought, and that's by taking it. "Some people," she continued, "prefer to hear feedback about what they are doing well, others prefer to hear only about opportunities for improvement, and some prefer a mixture of the two."

I relaxed a bit. I hadn't considered "compliments" feedback, just nice things people said to you if they wanted you to feel good or maybe as a prelude to a request they planned to make—or sometimes what was said to get you to work harder. (If I had been really working with the mirror concept *this* assumption would have certainly been revealing.)

"A mixture," I said, suddenly curious about what she might have seen that was positive and comforted by the neutrality of the question itself.

"You have a real gift for synthesis," she said. "You take what people say and give it back slightly modified, but in a way that allows them to consider their ideas freshly, a way that takes them beyond where they were going on their own. Did you learn that consciously or was it a gift you just came into the world with?"

This was interesting, I thought to myself. I wondered just what I was doing. She was defining it. She had given me a way to look at myself that would have been hard to grasp on my own.

"The way you work is very effective for dealing with information," Marilyn continued, "but it doesn't work too well when emotion is present."

I quickly considered whether I had adjusted my style, as it might have been advantageous to do, depending upon whether there was emotion present in a room or not, and realized with a start that I had not. In fact, with a sudden flash of awareness I realized I hadn't watched for emotion, only for information. I had stayed focused on whether the group was accomplishing what it had set out to do.

She continued, "Are you aware that you subtly steered the group in a different direction whenever emotional content was present?" I saw that what she said was accurate and applied to that day and times in the past. I was listening carefully now, barely breathing. "I'm just wondering," she said, "how comfortable you are with your own emotions. I would think that any work you might do in that area would surely enhance your already excellent skill at facilitation."

'This is feedback?' I thought to myself, seeing it demonstrated effectively for perhaps the first time. 'This is a gift to be treasured.'

We continued to talk about emotions, about how people respond when strong emotion is present. How their minds disengage so giving them information doesn't work. And how, when emotion is present, what is needed is simple acknowledgment and validation of their feelings and an expression of empathy for them. How it's important to

> **I discovered layer upon layer of negative self-judgments I had stacked against myself.**

use the same words they use when validating their emotions because they are in a feeling mode and even subtle word changes can make it seem that they haven't been heard. That feelings are feelings, and that what is helpful to people experiencing feelings is for them to know that it is okay for them to be having the feelings they are having. I had been creating the illusion of safety for myself by avoiding emotional situations in group meetings, but creating trust in such situations meant honoring, not ignoring feelings.

We talked, too, about how I could begin to work with myself in the emotional area by becoming more conscious of my own feelings and allowing myself to feel them, especially when my instinct was to push feelings like fear or sadness away.

Suddenly, without warning, Marilyn raised her arm up sharply in my direction and I instinctively moved back in my seat. "Like that," she said, "our natural response to unwanted feeling is very quick. Set an intention to stay aware of the sensations in your body that come forward when fear is present. And start collecting data to find out what happens just before a feeling occurs."

I remembered the first time I understood the sensation of anger in my body and how valuable that had been. I became very willing to do what she suggested.

Within months an array of words like frustration, irritation, fear, anxiety, righteousness, apathy, shame, and disappointment took on new meaning. I began to pinpoint what I truly felt in a given situation, to accu-

rately distinguish one feeling from another. I also saw the emotional patterns that existed between events and the feelings they triggered.

I had begun to carry a list of emotions; in times of confusion about what I truly felt, I would scan the list until something inside me said, "Yes, that's it!" I would then add a new word to my vocabulary of recognized emotional responses.

And I discovered layer upon layer of negative self-judgments I stacked against myself about having certain feelings—anger, envy, and despair, among them—at all. I saw that I had felt that having emotions like these was unacceptable, inappropriate, and just plain wrong. No wonder I had tuned them out. But they were just feelings. I forgave myself for judging myself harshly for having them and in so doing made it safer to feel such emotions.

I deepened my understanding of myself and my appreciation for attuning to the emotional life within me.

I became aware that my emotional strategy had been to navigate around—to avoid—strong negative emotion through control and manipulation of the environment around me, by trying to control other people's responses to me, or pretending that certain feelings didn't exist at all. In reaction to my growing awareness of this limiting pattern of behavior, I consciously invited learning opportunities to come forward; I made myself open to situations in which strong emotion might show up so I could learn from them. (I added, with a smile at my increasingly sophisticated use of the power of intention, that gentle learning would be preferred, if possible.) Feeling safer with my own emotions was beginning to make it safer to be around others who were feeling emotional.

Time passed. Then a consulting client, the head of a global transportation company, called expressing frustration at a seemingly endless string of calls from irate customers of his company.

"I'm beginning to think I just don't know what they want," he said, "and I'm getting sick and tired of being blasted by pissed-off customers who are never happy with us, even when we're probably the best operated company out there."

I considered the implications of what he had said. I had done work with him in the past regarding his company's dissatisfaction with a number of major US railroads. The company considered itself a customer of the railroads since it often shipped freight cross-country by rail, but had had a difficult time, in its view, being respected by the railroads—like having its ideas for improvement considered. I noted to myself that here was an example of the mirror concept operating company to company.

The president had a plan in mind for addressing customer satisfaction. He wanted to survey his customers about what their service priorities were. "We spend a lot of money on information systems," he said, "and I don't even know how important things like shipment tracking systems are to our customers versus everything else we could be spending money on."

"How come you don't know what's important to them?" I asked.

We had talked about this problem previously when he was trying to understand the corporate culture of railroads. I had shared my perception that companies like his, which were asset-focused (very concerned with the investments they made and the returns on them) often had a bit to learn about listening and responsiveness. A single-minded focus on assets kept the company internally oriented, often at the expense of customer relationships.

"You and I both know what your customers are going to say," I said to him. "They're going to say you don't listen to them. So we can do the survey you want and build the case with data, but it's not going to do any good unless you're prepared to address the underlying issues that are likely to surface. If you don't know your customers' priorities, then it's likely that there's not a lot of listening going on here. So let's assume we confirm that. Are you prepared to do something to address that conclusion? Because if you're not, you may be better off not even asking them for feedback."

> **We can bruise others with a "running-over-them" style, and this can limit our effectiveness.**

I noted the freedom that enabled me to talk directly to the president in this way. It meant that I had made progress. I had come to a place where I was able to call things as I saw them, which was evidence of my increased willingness to state my perceptions even at the risk of engaging other people's anger or upset.

We surveyed the company's customers about their customer-service needs and collected useful information and insights. We also discovered strong evidence that key customers considered the company "arrogant and hard to talk with," and on this basis alone a substantial portion of the company's business was in jeopardy. The president had agreed to deal with the consequences of our survey, so a couple of months later I found myself with a colleague in a room with over a dozen senior company players talking about listening skills.

As in many companies, this top layer of management

was dominated by individuals with results-driven person-
alities. DRIVERS.

The thing about drivers—and I am one—is that we're
interested in results. We care passionately about achievement, reaching goals, winning the race. Often our self-
esteem is intimately connected to accomplishment. It's
difficult for us to slow down to consider what others have
to say, especially when we get a whiff that what they're saying deviates from what we think will get us the result we
crave. We can bruise others with a "running-over-them"
style, and this can limit our effectiveness. (The converse is
also true; relationship-oriented individuals—people who
are focused on making sure everyone is heard and
involved—can lose sight of the desired results.)

I told the group that the key to improving customer
satisfaction was to slow down and listen to what their customers had to say.

"But if we slow down and listen," an operations manager said, "it will take too long. If we listen the way
you say, which is to stop and focus on what
the customer is saying, really listen, we're
never going to get everything done in the
time we have to do it, which they won't like

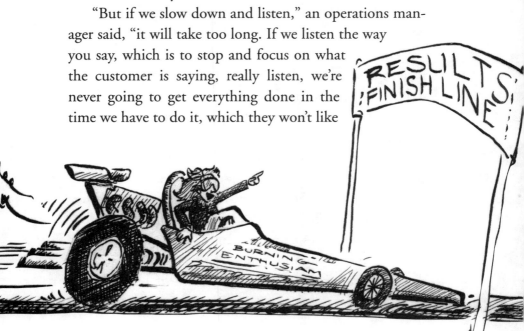

either. We won't achieve our goals, our objectives. We'll fall short of needed results."

"Plus," added a customer service supervisor, "customers don't always know what they're talking about. Sometimes they think we've done something wrong and it's really not our fault, but they don't want to hear that."

"Or," the head of pricing offered, "they could be trying to get us to do something that we can't do, like cut the rate beyond what we can afford." The president added, "It's like, the customers are doing their job, which is to beat us up on price and service, and we're doing our job, which is to get done what needs to get done and not get screwed in the process. I don't see how listening is going to do anything to change that, except everything will just take longer."

The heat was rising. Emotions were up. We were in borderline PNV territory. But I had a colleague with me who was great in the heat of emotional fervor so I would be fine.

He and I had been talking to the group about using a listening model called AVE (the letters stand for Acknowledge, Validate, and Empathize), a model of listening when emotional upset is present. It maintains that information just bounces off a person who is frustrated, angry, or in any way upset. The AVE model could help this company handle their irritated customers.

We explained this. "When customers are upset, they won't hear what you're saying," I told the group, "until they know that you are listening to them. They're in their feelings and can't process information. Until their feelings get validated, the customer won't be able to hear the information you want to give them, so giving it won't do much good."

I looked around the room. Blank, rigid stares.

"I can understand how frustrating it is," my colleague said smoothly. "You're on the phone, they're upset, maybe yelling. It's not your fault, they're being unreasonable, and you're being pulled in a million directions. You have five calls on hold and a lot of work to get done and you just want to get off the phone and get on with it. That has to be a really tough, unpleasant, frustrating situation."

"Yeah, it is tough," said the operations manager, noticeably relaxing, softening. He had been heard and understood. The tension in the room noticeably eased.

It was AVE in action. And in seeing the model work, as it just had, I became aware that I had more to learn before I could apply it instinctively. I had been trying to give the group information before I had stopped to listen to them, before I had heard them.

"So who wants to be the customer?" I asked. "Who can get good and irate?"

The operations manager laughed. "Well I'm kind of into it," he said, "I guess I might as well keep going with it."

"Great," my colleague said. "Who's willing to be the person taking the call? We're going to role-play this." The regional sales manager stuck up his hand and came up to the front of the room.

I leaned over the shoulder of the person pretending to take the call, and my colleague got in position behind the "customer." "Okay," my partner said, "you're the customer, a load is late and that lateness is about to shut the plant down, which isn't going to make anyone happy. You don't want excuses, you want the situation fixed and now!"

The dialogue began:

Customer: Hey George, I'm really upset here. We got a late load and it's the second time this month. We can't have that! I don't know what the problem is but I'm about to have a plant shut-down here and damn it, that's going to be a headache. You guys need to get your friggin' act together. I don't know why you're having these problems but this is just not acceptable!

Company: Well, I don't know what happened, but you need to calm down. There's no reason to come unglued. That's not going to get the truck there any faster and I don't really appreciate being screamed at right now.

I turned and looked at the person playing the customer. "Do you feel heard?" I asked him.

"No," he said. "I feel put down and not paid attention to. I'm really mad!" he elaborated, "and you're making it seem like it's no big deal. I'm just getting madder by the minute."

"Okay," my partner said, "that's good feedback. So use the AVE model, let him know you hear he's upset, that you understand. Try it again."

Company: I hear you're really upset and I can sure understand that. If I had a situation on my hands with a plant about to shut down, I'd be furious too.

I turned to the guy playing the customer, "How about now? Are you feeling heard now?"

"It's amazing," he said, "I'm still very concerned, but I'm ready to talk about options and figure out what we can do. I'm ready to hear what you have to say," he said to his partner in the dialogue.

AVE's value had become clear.

We spent the rest of the afternoon role-playing, running through additional exercises and talking about the challenge of listening when high emotion is present. We talked about what it felt like to be listened to, how listening shifted emotional energy and provided the opportunity for productive conversation that in the end took less time to resolve disputes. A breakthrough came when the group realized that listening, taking in what was being said, didn't mean having to agree with any explanations, events, or facts; it just meant validating and understanding someone's emotional experience as real for them. It would take time and practice for the group members (and me) to master AVE skills, but willingness was present. We had begun.

It was a next step for me, too. Validating my own emotional experience was a richly rewarding process and one of the more difficult challenges I have faced as an adult. When I am consciously experiencing strong emotion, surrendering to it can make me feel profoundly vulnerable, as if I may literally shatter and fly apart.

But it's not the emotional experience itself but my negative judgment of it that causes the pain. When I experience any emotion and judge that experience as wrong, not safe, or that I'm wrong or bad for having it, I can feel cut to the quick. However, there's a way out: forgiveness of the negative judgment—giving up my desire to condemn myself for having had the experience.

Such forgiveness is healing. It expresses a depth of natural compassion for the pain we experience as we judge ourselves and others as wrong. Withholding negative judgment doesn't mean that we stop evaluating situations or stop knowing that actions have consequences; rather, it allows us to be gentler with ourselves when we are learning. Embracing learning is a whole lot easier than resisting it by wishing an event had gone otherwise—that somehow we should have or could have done it differently. If we could have, we would have. Forgiveness is about compassionate acceptance that in that moment, for where we were at the time, we did the very best we could.

A few years later, a new client called. His company was struggling with how to get sixteen autonomous divisions to agree on measuring customer-service performance. For weeks the client and I had flown around the country, having meeting after meeting with the various divisions, and it started to dawn on me that in no way was the project budget designed for this amount of face-to-face. So I decided to propose a phone conference the following week (instead of another meeting between New Jersey, Chicago, and Dallas company divisions) to discuss a download of data from their computer to our consulting firm.

I know Steve, the project manager, isn't going to like my plan—he always favors face-to-face meetings—and I'm nervous about the discussion. But I tell myself I'm blessed; I've got a clear case of PNV on my hands with someone who is not only a driver but a perfectionist and I'm going to learn a lot!

I call Steve and tell him my plan. "I don't know," he says, his temperature clearly rising in reaction to my suggestion, "I see this as crucial, critical—if we don't get the data, we're not successful. I just think it is not worth the risk of not doing this face-to-face. It has to go a lot better in person than over the phone. I just don't see how it can work that way."

We're on the phone, but I can sense his throbbing neck veins through the line. I start to get a bit annoyed. We don't have an unlimited budget for travel here; what does he expect me to do?

"We can do this project any way you want, Steve," I say tersely. "We can do it the way it was planned, with little travel. Look at the budget; the money isn't there. Or we can do the meetings with travel and in person, but then we can't stay within the original budget."

Steve becomes a tornado, gathering arguments to support his position, spinning higher and higher emotionally. And suddenly I get it: I'm not hearing a word he's saying.

I stop and take a breath. "So what's your concern?" I say to him gently, suddenly more calm. I'm trying not to make his reaction wrong, trying not to make myself wrong either for not having heard him.

"What is it that you really want to hear me say right now?" I ask him.

"I just want to hear you say that you co-own responsibility for getting the data," he says. "I don't want to have that responsibility solely on my shoulders and then not do everything possible to ensure that getting the data happens."

> **I saw that I was dealing with anger, with PNVs, in a new, productive way.**

I woke up to the reasonableness of his concern. I recognized that he wasn't just trying to push me around. His response came out of his need for the project's success, which I wanted too. I also saw how he had used anger as a cover for his anxiety about failing. I could relate to that fear, I felt it too. We talked further, but in a different way now, aiming toward the same objective. Our objective.

Later, I went over what had happened between us. I saw that, in light of his anger, I was trying to make Steve wrong. Then, seeing that, I had stepped back and was able to listen to what Steve was really saying. I saw that I was dealing with anger, with PNVs, in a new, productive way.

Years earlier, Matt's anger—his PNVs—had just been upsetting; it had incapacitated me because I wasn't yet in touch with my anger and my underlying self-judgments. Once I was, I was able to be in the presence of anger but still feel safe. I was learning to deal with anger more effectively. It wasn't complete nirvana, but it felt like I was on my way. It felt good.

I'm still waiting for the day when the sight or sound of someone's PNVs automatically brings forward compassion on my part. And I know that the next step toward that place starts inside of me, it starts with compassion for myself.

Et tu, Brute?

Embracing a
Perilous Path
Toward
Productivity
and
Effectiveness

▼

Problems
cannot be solved
at the same level
of awareness
that created them.

—

ALBERT EINSTEIN

CHAPTER 3

Et tu, Brute?

EARLY in the establishment of our consulting practice we were asked by a large organization to lead an internal team of individuals who had been given a huge challenge: reduce company manufacturing, distribution, and inventory costs by forty percent, creating a savings of about $120 million annually. We were asked to participate because of the expertise in analysis, problem solving, and project management we had demonstrated on prior assignments. Other members of the team had a similar record of achievement and cross-functional experience.

But the company was asking for something more than cost reduction. The president also wanted to develop an in-house group of change agents who, after the project's completion, would be funneled into other areas of the company to lead new projects of a similar nature. It was this company's approach to continuous quality improvement—an ongoing search for ways to achieve greater effectiveness. Rather than implement a standardized continuous improvement program based on the experience of others, the company wanted to discover its own path to quality.

We gathered for a get-acquainted meeting—the project leader, the newly formed and freshly important group of internal experts, and us. Linda, the project leader, laid out the thinking behind the decision to form the group, talked about why each person had been chosen to be part of the team, and then summarized the specific goals for the project—paramount among them the forty percent cost reduction. This target came as news to many in the room; Linda and the company president, Jack, had agreed to it earlier in the week.

As Linda revealed the targeted cost reduction of forty percent, the expressions on the faces of those in the room ranged from a dazed glaze to panic to hostility to excitement. (The latter belonged to my partner—he loves a challenge.)

The sidebar agreement on the goal was not the only setup going on. The project leader had shared with me that in reality she was not sure that all individuals on the team had the experience to do the job. She felt confident that with us working behind the scenes organizing the data collection, analyzing the information, and directing the overall process, the job could get done. She thought this was best left unspoken—and I recognized a familiar pattern. Clients often explain the role of consultants differently to different people and so I wasn't especially concerned. Linda believed that to get the president to agree to her plan to use external consultants, she had to position the internal team as fully in charge of the project. To us, she had said, "You know how we work. Just do your thing."

At the time, I perceived and understood Linda's fear

('*Will others recognize the value I contribute?*') and her strategy of getting this need met ('*I want to be perceived as the creator of great value*'). If I had been aware of the Piper Principle and its assumption that a leader's fears and concerns show up as distortions along the way to the goal like a hall-of-mirrors, I would have been on the lookout for the way this could play out in the project. I might also have reflected on whether the concern I had identified was Linda's...or mine.

Piper Principle — 'pi-pər prin(t)-s(ə)pl — n. (circa 2000 <Judith Anderson):

1: What troubles a person most about a situation, a boss, a colleague, an employee, a customer, a vendor actually reveals an aspect of themselves (an underlying fear or concern) they don't yet see; a blind spot.

2: Underlying fears and concerns of leaders, and the unconscious way in which they protect themselves from them, show up in parable form as organizational barriers or blocks to achieving whatever goals are set.

3: When aggravation or blocks show up, a person can pay the piper, investigate the blind spot, and resolve the fear and concern—or blame others. Unproductive patterns repeat until you pay the piper.

One individual spoke, seemingly for everyone: "The forty percent goal is impossible," he said. "It can't be done. If it could be done, it would have already been done. A forty percent cost reduction is too much—it's plain ridiculous. The head of manufacturing isn't an idiot, there just can't be that much slack in the system. We're going to look foolish when we're unable to realize the goal."

Heads nodded.

My consulting partner piped up. "I have an idea," he said, "let's prove that—that it can't be done. We'll learn something equally important in that process."

The cost reduction objective was a stretch goal, one that posits a big jump. To attain a stretch goal, you must think differently than you normally do, even radically. And that's the point. Fine-tuning existing procedures works— you can achieve a ten-to-fifteen percent improvement in a given area by tweaking the system that is in place. But radical change demands radical thinking. You have to be creative. Stretch goals stimulate creativity. They force new thinking, new ways of looking at the system, new approaches. New thinking was what the president wanted. He had set a big goal to inspire that type of thinking.

"I mean, think about it," my partner continued. "What would have to change around here for forty percent of the work and related costs to go away and have product availability goals met? How could we prove that *isn't* possible?"

Minds started to turn, mental engines hummed. I guessed everyone was thinking about specific wasteful activities that might be eliminated. A few bold ideas were offered that were interesting to consider. Possibilities started to emerge. One person said, "It might actually be harder to prove that a forty percent cost reduction *isn't* possible. Maybe it can be done. It would be an awesome win!" When the group started imagining the win, the goal became at least sixty-five percent believable. (Sixty-five percent is the magic number meaning a stretch goal is somewhat believable—in the realm of possibility, but not a "slam dunk".) Just that quickly we were off toward realizing it.

The group had successfully faced one of the major obstacles to becoming a team—buy-in toward the goal. (We collaborate because *we* want to achieve *our* goal.) You need a shared vision of a goal to collaborate regarding the best route to get there. When there is no shared goal, (or shared enemy) to rally around, there is little basis for group cohesion.

A misstep on the road to buy-in is bypassing a discussion of *what* a group's goal is and jumping into a discussion of *how* to reach it. In these cases, people leap over the *"what"* and go right to the *"how,"* often with radically different approaches to achieving a goal. Some of this disagreement is productive; it helps us buy into a goal to consider what is required to reach it. But often when there is not a meeting of the minds about the goal, debate goes to an unproductive level and we start making other team members "wrong" for their approach to the goal. Often when I can untangle disagreements like this, I discover that there are individuals who articulate the goal differently, and are therefore moving toward different visions. For each person, his or her own approach makes sense.

A subtle variation of this is withholding commitment to the goal until it is clear whether or not the goal is achievable. An interesting strategy! This is fear of failure masked by rationality.

Another pattern that complicates the buy-in process is the belief that we don't need to commit to a particular goal before we start to work toward something—that we'll discover what we can accomplish as we go along. Non-linear thinkers—spontaneous idea generators as opposed to those who proceed logically step-by-step—might prefer the leave-it-open approach. So might free-spirited adventurers who want to keep all options available, even about where they're headed, as long as possible. However, ambiguity in a business drains resources and gives individuals a justification for placing individual priorities over shared goals.

Passionate commitment to a goal is a process of internal alignment. We tap into our wisdom and experience to check out whether a particular goal is something that we want to achieve and are aligned with. We identify the goal as something that is challenging but within the realm of possibility and we see that it will tap our talents and allow us to grow in the process. We may need to know why the goal is important to others, we may have questions about resources, we may need information about how we will be supported, but commitment to the goal is as much a search of the heart as it is a search of the mind. In the end, we "choose in" or "choose out." (And if we are committed to learning, either choice will provide ample opportunity to learn.)

To get to passionate commitment to a shared goal, concerns about the goal as well as how people work together to achieve it need to be expressed and heard. What my partner was really saying when he suggested changing the project objective was, "I'm okay with you being concerned about failure. If I thought I was being set up to fail, I'd be concerned too. I'm with you—let's set this up for success!" If we are to passionately engage the heart of a team, then whatever underlies holding back needs to be addressed.

This isn't to suggest that strong leadership isn't needed as well. Leaders can inspire others to accomplish more than they thought possible. One of the reasons to collaborate is that as a group, we often become more willing to risk more, to shoot for more aggressive goals. An effective leader can inspire others to follow him or her toward a purposeful objective. In fact, that's what happened in our group. Linda had passion. She believed in the forty percent goal and she believed it could be done. Her belief was contagious.

Everyone on the team had a track-record of success. One individual was a scientist who had directed several successful research projects. Another had been responsible for designing several of the company's manufacturing processes. A third came from marketing. Ours was a true cross-functional effort that brought together an array of individual backgrounds and diverse experiences to address a significant opportunity for the company. The team was off to a good start: focused, energized and committed. In terms of team development, it had "formed".

The project had come about because of the company's history of problems with product shortages. The company would often be out of product and weeks away from re-supply. Or they found themselves throwing product away because it was overstocked and outdated. Sometimes these events occurred almost simultaneously; the company would discard outdated product and then run short a few weeks later.

> **The team was off to a good start: focused, energized and committed. In terms of team development, it had "formed".**

I had attended several meetings at which Jack, the president, kept attempting to clarify what was causing these inventory problems. Explanations were offered about equipment breaking down and vendor materials failing quality inspection, but no insight was offered about how performance could be improved. "It's the nature of equipment to break," the head of manufacturing had said self-protectively, relying on the explanation he used whenever a key product was out of stock.

Jack had been frustrated by the lack of enthusiasm for change in the company. "I want you to make waves," he had said to Linda when he authorized the project. "I want you and the team to challenge the status quo." Jack wanted the project to deliver the message that he had not been successful delivering one-on-one.

Linda embraced her role as a change-agent, someone responsible for altering entrenched patterns of operation. She didn't need to be a popular person. In fact, she expected resistance and Jack provided the armor. "This project is important to our success," the president had told Linda at its outset. "Don't be concerned about operations not liking what you're doing. That's the point—they're comfortable with the way things are. But I'll be behind you."

Linda shared her confidence in Jack's support with the team. Everyone knew she and Jack had a good relationship—he had counted on her for special projects in the past. We got started with our eyes open, feet on the ground, and pointed in the direction of a solution. Once the group had bought into the possibility of the forty percent goal, my partner and I worked with them to develop a detailed plan and approach for realizing it.

Our company had worked with Linda before, but not with the other team members, so it was slow-going initially to get various responsibilities sorted out, to get everyone clear on individual roles in the project. We advocated a simple four-step project framework: What? Why? How? Now? (What is the goal? Why is it important? How do we get there? What needs to be done now?) Other team members liked a more complex "seven-step" model. Defining our approach to the project took us deep into the "storming" phase and we emerged more confident as a team and even more committed to the goal.

Members of the group discussed openly which values we shared—such as keeping commitments and being honest with one another. We even hung signs around our meeting room listing our values and protocols. These symbolized our commitment to one another. Often in the heat of a discussion, one of the team members would leap up, slap one of the posted signs and say, pointing to "honesty,"

for example, "I'm talking about *this,* are we being honest right now?" Openness and commitment drew us together and roles sorted themselves out. We were in what is known as stage three of team development, norming, in which group members affirm norms or rules to guide group activity and increase their commitment to the goal and each other.

The company had been using MRP, a standard manufacturing resource planning tool that predicts how much production is necessary to avoid product shortages. The system also identifies the raw materials needed to make product so these can be purchased ahead of time, and schedules products through the various production steps to ensure that company capacity is efficiently used.

The MRP system works, but it's enormously complex. Each person in the manufacturing process works with only one aspect of it (the system is ultimately responsible for linking all the pieces together). What is difficult to do with the system, however, is diagnose a problem in it. Few people using the system understand exactly how what they do with the system affects everyone else using the system. Thus, while MRP systems, and others like them, help manage complex situations, they're also perfect for hiding problems.

Early in the project, as one of his bold ideas, my partner suggested to the team that the company stop using the MRP system and do planning and scheduling of current orders "by hand." Fewer than a dozen or so new manufacturing orders were generated each day, so it would be easy, he maintained, to track them. With a "by hand" approach, the company's planners and schedulers would understand the manufacturing process better, recognize where improvements might be made, and eliminate the work that was required to correct errors in the system. It wasn't a practical sell, really—the idea of replacing the new with the old was counter-intuitive—but it represented the kind of out-of-the-box thinking that started the team exploring imaginative ideas.

"Here's what we're going to do," my partner said, "we're going to take the orders generated tomorrow—then, every day following, we're going to look up those orders as they proceed through the system and track what's happening with them. We're going to document everything the system says is happening to an order."

The other members of the team didn't buy it. It seemed like a lot of work; there must be, they insisted, a way of extracting the data automatically. And they dug in their heels.

The path to the creation of a high performance team is circuitous. Teams often drop back to earlier stages—in this case storming. Conflict is part of the creative process—it can be a useful stage if it means individuals care about outcome. Ideally, what is needed are effective collaborative skills for resolving conflicts creatively so that all members stay fully engaged. We weren't quite there yet. My partner and I viewed ourselves as having the experience to know what to do, and the other team members as needing to pitch in where and when they could to assist with what needed doing. (This attitude on our part was, as I saw later, one more example of betrayal.)

"It's not just the data we want," my partner said. "We want to start seeing the way the system itself is being used so we can understand what's going on in it. We want to crawl around inside it, to start thinking about the way the system thinks and the way the people who use it think."

He chose two of the team members that afternoon, including the Ph.D. researcher scientist, to focus on data extraction, sat down with them, and showed them what he wanted done daily to track the orders. After an hour or so the researcher stood up and threw her pencil down. "This is ridiculous!" she said. "I'm not doing this work. You're not using my education and talent at all. You're asking me to copy numbers off a computer screen and saying that that's a reasonable use of my capabilities. You need to figure out something for me to do that uses my talent."

"I'll make you a deal," my partner said. "You do this for five days and then tell me what you think. Once you get the pattern down, it should only take an hour or two each day to track the orders. My guess is that we need to do this for a month so we have time to see orders go all the way through the system. But if you don't think it's valuable after five days, if you don't feel like you are contributing by learning something important, then I'll do it."

The researcher scientist agreed.

Sometimes in business there's a point of view that says expressing strong emotion is not appropriate, not professional. When an emotional outburst appears, the belief is that something went awry, and a return to an "orderly" state, one in which such an outburst won't occur, is desirable. Earlier in my career, I often had that point of view: outbursts meant something had gone wrong.

High-performance teams—groups like ours—can be freer where emotional expression is concerned. Passion is expected. We're all in this together, is the prevailing group belief; if something is bothering someone, he or she is expected to say what it is. It doesn't matter if that feeling isn't expressed perfectly. If the group is going to meet its goal, there can't be holding back. As emotional skills become stronger, feelings can be articulated rather than acted out. But, at our stage of development, we were glad to have feedback delivered any which way. A more respectful, peer-to-peer relationship soon emerged.

The hand-tracking experiment proceeded. After three days of system watching, the two people assigned to extract data about orders were puzzled; what the MRP system said was happening with orders didn't make sense. Out of the blue, the size of a manufacturing order (the number of units to be produced) would somehow change. In one case an order dropped completely off the production schedule. What was going on? Maybe we weren't reading the data correctly. Maybe we didn't understand the system and how to extract information from it correctly.

A meeting between the team and operations was set up. During the meeting, it became clear that the order planner and the order scheduler were operating independently and had different objectives. The planner, whose job it was to review inventory levels and inform schedulers about when orders needed to be filled, was working to make sure inventory levels didn't drop too low. The scheduler, on the other hand, wanted order sizes that were economical to produce and a pattern of production that maximized labor and machine utilization.

Something else was going on. The scheduler had his own way of organizing data about each manufacturing order that made scheduling an efficient process for *him.* To that end, he copied certain information off manufacturing orders and put it in his own format (a spreadsheet)—with one critical exception—he didn't enter the date the order was due. Scheduling was rewarded for minimizing production costs, not meeting due dates. The scheduler didn't understand how crucial that date was to inventory control and the entire production process, because the date wasn't important in his sub-process. Thus, only when inventory levels dropped low enough for a product to be placed on a "low-stock list" would it then be scheduled for production (with no time for corrective action if machines broke down).

> **Blinded to what was being set up by our unconscious insensitivity to people's feelings and excited by our progress, the team really revved up.**

In fact, because of the way scheduling was handled, so many products were on the low-stock report that the report, rather than the orders from planning, became the driver of what was scheduled. This explained the pattern of inventory problems the company president had seen for so long but that no one could explain— the very problem that had triggered the project in the first place.

The two data extractors, excited by the insight, pointed out that if the scheduler and the planner huddled for an hour each morning and compared plans, both might be better off. The planner could help the scheduler stay focused on the due dates and the scheduler could push up orders a few days to help keep the manufacturing cost structure optimized.

The meetings we had suggested take place between the planner and scheduler started to happen the following week. In the team's glee at having been able to bring about meaningful change, however, we disregarded the impact of the way we had communicated our desire for the meeting to the people involved. We drew attention to the fact that the inventory problems were due to something manufacturing had overlooked and that we had seen. This "zap", fed by the need to be recognized for bringing influential ideas to the table, boomeranged.

Blinded to what was being set up by our unconscious insensitivity to people's feelings and excited by our progress, the team really revved up. We started believing that we could actually reach the forty percent cost reduction goal.

On the interpersonal side, team members continued to learn about one another's strengths, discovering who needed what kind of support. Our method of tracking commitments and keeping focused on the project goal was working—each person understood his or her role. Our creativity and "group think" were generating lots of ideas.

We decided to list every cost-reduction idea we had come up with so far and do a "quick and dirty" one-hour analysis of the potential impact each idea might have. We would then know which ideas were in the ballpark, could rank them, then improve the analysis of those ideas that seemed to be most promising.

The results were quite helpful. We didn't have the forty percent cost reduction in the bag, with its $120 million savings, but we had a lot of three to five million dollar cost reduction ideas. We had entered the final "performing" stage of team development, the one in which a group is able to work collaboratively and creatively toward shared goals.

For example, we looked at the company's organizational layers and found that many managers had only one or two individuals reporting to them. In theory, doubling the number of reports, and concurrently reducing the number of managers, would save the company more than $20 million a year. We were so focused on realizing the forty percent goal while we idea-stormed that we forgot that real people would have real concerns about what change would mean. It wasn't on our radar screen. We had been directed to ignore these reactions and we were content to oblige this mandate.

> As we began to raise specific ideas to operations, resistance flared up.

As we began to raise specific ideas to operations, resistance flared up. This took the form of confrontations in meetings held to review our progress with operations. Operations began to suggest the entire project wasn't being done right, suggesting that the team was like a run-a-way horse galloping at full speed toward the edge of a cliff.

The team shrugged its collective shoulders at the resistance; we had been told it was inevitable. In fact, resistance was taken by the group to signal that we were doing a good job at challenging the status quo; hadn't doing so been the president's mandate? Our ability to prove we could achieve the goal was what mattered to us. Certainly it mattered more than our relationship with the production people and their concerns. We told ourselves that a zealous commitment to the goal was justified because it kept the project moving forward. So we kept going.

I made a weak suggestion about addressing the struggle between operations and the team in a different way, offering that Jack, the key managers in operations, and the team should get together for an open dialogue about what the team had been asked to do and why. Maybe we needed to make a decision together about how to proceed that would address the resistance and engage production's buy-in.

In retrospect it seemed likely that Jack hadn't revealed to the head of manufacturing the necessity of shaking things up. In any case, I felt it was time to get all concerns on the table and decide what was actually best for the company. After all, it was manufacturing, not us, that was going to have to make any changes work.

And something in me wanted to hear from Jack directly on the subject of ignoring any resistance we might encounter in trying to reach our goals. Jack's stance in this regard had seemed out of character to me. I had always viewed him as a consensus manager. I was having increasing difficulty with the idea that an indication of the project's success was, as Linda said Jack had stated, the existence of organizational conflict.

Linda didn't like the idea of our meeting with Jack—especially our participation in it. She and we knew that everyone on the team was contributing, but it was also true that my partner and I, with her, were leading the group. We were playing a big role. She expressed concern that if we met with Jack, it might appear that we, "outside" consultants, were playing a more important role than she had communicated. She had sold the project to Jack on the basis that the internal team would drive the project and this perception therefore needed to be maintained.

Why was I unwilling to trust my experience?

I wasn't lined up with this, but I nonetheless chose to accommodate Linda. So I dropped the idea of meeting with Jack, but as I did, I recognized a familiar sinking feeling that I couldn't quite label. Why had I backed down when I had a strong intuition that we should be getting everyone together? Why was I unwilling to trust my experience as my partner had done when he held his ground on the value of collecting detailed data about a few sample orders?

One aspect of my personality that I had been
ashamed of until then and often attempted to disguise,
was a desire for recognition and applause—a wish that
my contributions be seen and appreciated. The reason I
thought I had a handle on Linda's fears and concerns was
that they mirrored my own. I half suspected that part of
the reason for my suggesting
the meeting with Jack was
that I wanted an audience,
wanted my true role to be
seen, that of someone who
asks crucial questions and
gets hidden agendas up and
on the table. I knew I had the
skills to do these things, and

that a candid discussion with Jack and operations was
what the project needed. Still, I doubted my motivation.
Was I just tired of having to pretend to be playing the
"minor" role as Linda had set it up? Was my desire to have
the meeting with Jack what the project needed or what *I*
needed?

The familiar sinking feeling signaled that I wasn't
trusting myself. Could I trust myself to know my true feelings and desires? Given the uncertainty, how could I hold
my ground in service to the project's success? I didn't feel
on solid ground and so I backed away from my experience
and my instincts. I continued to pretend that the "desig-
nated" role we had didn't matter to me. In doing so, I did
not see my own self-betrayal, nor my role in the deception
game that had been unfolding.

There were, it seemed, more pressing issues to address.

We were nearing the project's mid-point. To reach our goal, we had been using a management technique my partner had devised, creatively titled the Half-Life Process. It's a great technique for producing results on-time and on-budget when you're engaged in a creative endeavor and you don't know exactly what the end result will look like. When you're constructing a building, in contrast, coordination is key, and the Critical Path Method, which establishes times and task interdependencies, works well. But in a creative process, tomorrow's plan depends on what was discovered today. What is needed is a way to keep a handle on the work, so that promising ideas ultimately revealed as unproductive don't absorb too many resources and too much time.

What often happens in projects like ours is that solutions and insights come too late. It's only when you synthesize and summarize information that you see what critical drivers are important and know what additional information would be valuable to validate ideas. When this happens late in a project, for example, when you're pulling together the final recommendations for cost reductions, there can be no time to react to what has been learned, so results are not as good as they could have been.

Using the half-life method, you pretend you have only half the time you actually do to achieve what needs to be done. This artificial deadline forces you to cut off research and document findings earlier than you would normally; nonetheless, a good deal of data collection and learning still takes place. At the end of the artificial time allotted, you take a breath, see what has been learned and identify what "conclusion" you've arrived at. Often, crucial insights are reached in time to test with additional data. This becomes the focus for the "second half" of the project. The artificial end-point acts as a natural constraint on the level of detail that can be pursued and helps ensure the project is completed "on time" with sufficient data to support key conclusions.

We began to construct our half-life synthesis in relation to the forty percent goal, which meant summarizing cost reduction opportunities we believed made sense. We had diagnosed the cost structure—we knew where the big costs were—and the forty percent cost reduction now seemed fully in the realm of possibility. But as we looked at the group's cost reduction ideas listed on a single sheet of paper, we saw something new. What emerged was an idea that would enable us to implement many changes synergistically. Instead of organizing production around three phases managed by different groups—bulk production of key components, production of finished product, and packaging (as they were now)—we would propose individual, integrated production processes around similar packaging concepts. Those lines would operate as teams and this would create greater opportunity for continuous improvement in the future.

When we presented the "half-life" summary of our thinking to operations, each team member laid out specific ideas and led discussions in the areas in which each had developed the greatest expertise. Everyone on the team did an excellent job of answering questions and clarifying understanding. It was evident that our group was performing with a high level of expertise, had developed creative ideas, understood the data that led to their conclusions and owned the results. Their command of details was impressive. This was what Linda had wanted to create and its realization was a significant accomplishment for her.

The reaction came in two waves. The first took the form of a genuine desire by operations management to understand the data and the conclusions we'd reached. When they questioned facts, it was in a spirit of wanting to understand our thinking rather than to challenge us. This surprising but welcomed change in attitude looked like the type of open dialogue we had been wanting. Together the group mapped out what additional information in the "post-half-life" phase would be most illuminating.

Unbeknownst to us, however, the attitude adjustment belied a second response that was already underway. The game of "betrayal hopscotch" we were all seemingly engaged in took on more overt and sophisticated strategies on the part of operations management.

Two days after our half-life meeting, Jack announced the hiring of Frank as new head of production operations.

> **Bewilderment, then a sense of deep betrayal hit the members of the team.**

He came to the company with a highly qualified track record in managing change. In addition to his broad responsibilities in operations, Frank would replace Linda as the project team's leader. In explaining the reason for this to Linda, Jack had said, "It's really important that we get buy-in in order to implement your recommendations, and bringing Frank onboard is the way to do it. I know you're only half way through the project—Frank's presence will ensure that the second half builds-in the reality and experience necessary to make sure your conclusions are bought into and implemented."

Bewilderment, then a sense of deep betrayal hit the members of the team. They had been told by Jack not to worry about buy-in; now their leader was being removed so buy-in could take place. The team had expected Jack to encourage management to consider our recommendations; it had placed its faith in Jack's support. Now someone was being brought in to run the team who didn't understand the way the team worked. This surprising replacement of the team's leadership was a painful rupture of trust.

Some team members went to speak to Jack directly to express their feelings and share their concerns. Some members put their response down in a memo to him. And some decided to keep quiet so as to not risk jeopardizing whatever future Jack had in store for them after the project ended. For our part, we breathed a mild sigh of relief that at least the project was going to continue and that we were going to remain involved, not a certainty considering the nature of such projects and Linda's removal. Not only were we emotionally invested in the team but, practically speaking, our time had been fully occupied, and to stop now would mean looking for a new client. Hiring Frank had been a brutal way to get the issue of buy-in on the table. But, perhaps he would be of value

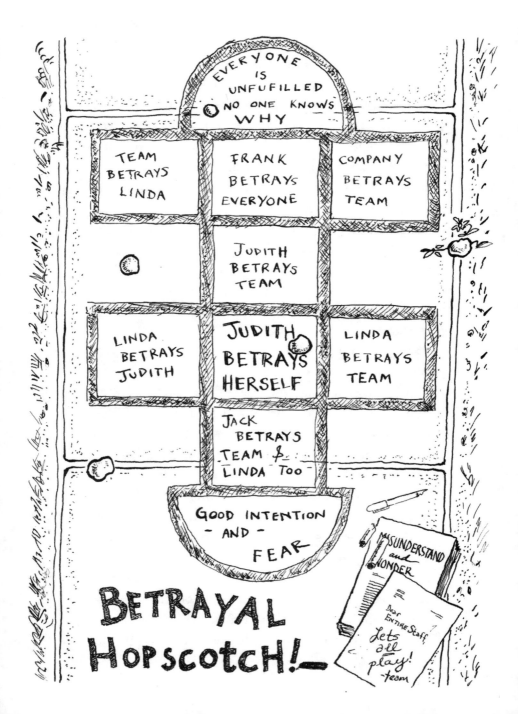

to the team and even greater success lay just ahead.

Still, I wanted to understand what had happened, and especially, what I could do differently next time. I knew there was something I had missed that would have made it possible to facilitate a more successful experience for everyone. What was it? The more I thought about it, the more it seemed that what had happened was pre-destined; Jack had never shown much support for the team. He had made commitments early on, but then had nearly dropped out of sight. Looking back, I saw that the tension between all parties had been stretched too tight for too long; the break between operations and Linda and the team was the result of what had taken place up to that point.

> **When we can't see the interplay between an inner dilemma and the outer struggle, it means a "blind spot" is operating.**

But I couldn't quite catch what my role in the outcome had been. From the perspective of the Piper Principle, I guessed intellectually that self-trust had to be a factor because a betrayal pattern was underway. I had used this principle effectively before; to see a barrier or challenge more clearly, it helped to consider the external challenge as a mirror of an inner struggle or dilemma. In the past, this concept had helped me untangle "side-swipes," to see how a dynamic had been set up and understand my role in it. When we can't see the interplay between an inner dilemma and the outer struggle, it means a "blind spot" is operating. At that time, I couldn't see what it was. For myself, what that meant was that there was something quite helpful yet to learn.

Once Frank was in charge of the project, the ground rules changed considerably. At his first meeting with the team, Frank did most of the talking. He outlined a number of seminars he had attended, what he had learned at them, books he had read, and his ideas about teamwork. The team had lived and breathed much of what he talked about for the past six months. A couple of attempts were made by the group to let Frank know about their first-hand experience of what he was saying, but these were half-heartedly expressed. It was clear Frank had a plan. I wanted to know what it was.

At one point Frank interrupted a summary of next steps underway. "All that's fine with me," he said, "you'll find I'm not a micro-manager. I'm not going to change what's working; all I care about is the big picture, what we're trying to do. As for buy-in, I think I can help with that. I'm new, but I know operations people, I know how it works in production: that's my job—to get the buy-in to happen."

I tried to put a good face on things. Frank probably could get buy-in, I decided. And the not-micromanaging business sounded good. The team would be left alone to continue to do its work, I told myself, and Frank would provide a missing piece.

Then Frank pulled out an article he said he had read recently on cycle-time reduction and told us what a boon it had been to many organizations in achieving competitive advantage. Cycle-time is the period between starting something and finishing it. Anything can be looked at in this way—the period that elapses from the development of a new product until it's on the shelf, for example, or the time it takes from the moment a customer places an order to receipt of the product. Frank wanted the second half of the project to focus on cutting manufacturing cycle-time in half—reducing the time it took between making product and its shipment to a customer. He said that cutting out time would remove fat and unproductive activity, reducing waste and cost in the process.

My partner, who has an uncanny ability to cut to the chase, said, "Well, I don't quite see how that can be. Most time gets added into the manufacturing process when products and materials are sitting still, waiting to be utilized. But most cost gets added in when activity—handling and moving product—is taking place. So I don't quite see how you're going to get rid of costs by getting rid of sitting-around time. You might improve service to the customer if you're out of product and it doesn't take so long to make it, or you might uncover some inefficiencies. I can see how cycle-time reduction might be a good thing, but it doesn't seem like the thing to focus on if what you want is a big cost reduction."

Frank didn't like this challenge. "Well, you may not have the experience that I have in manufacturing or in this business," he said. "I've been doing a lot of reading, and cycle-time reduction strategies are the leading-edge thing, so you might not have come across them before. Now, if you don't want to be involved with this, that's fine, but it's where we're going to focus—and everything in my experience tells me that it's the right focus for us."

My partner and I looked at each other, then at the team members. Frank had a compelling track record. It was quite possible he knew more than we did, that he had great instincts for what steps needed to be taken. We already had much of the data that would be required. It seemed like the choice was to cooperate or be dismissed from a project half-way through. What options were there? Why not give it a go? In time, Frank would recognize the value we could contribute and maybe then we could better influence his thinking about the project.

This time, I barely noticed the sinking feeling.

The team kicked back into gear and created a detailed picture of cycle-time in relation to the manufacturing process of the company's largest product, which was manufactured in a stand-alone facility. We did this by synthesizing data from numerous automated and manual systems and tracking raw materials through the production process by lot number. We identified ways to reduce cycle-time by a significant amount (forty percent) and the benefits to customers of doing this were clear. Updating our approach, one of the members of the team worked closely behind the scenes to successfully gain buy-in from the plant manager. But not many cost-reduction opportunities were identified; our efforts hadn't improved our understanding of how to achieve our initial goal.

When we presented our results to Frank, he shook his

head. "Well, I can see that you have done a lot of work here," he said, "but the results are just not what I expected. I mean, they just aren't consistent with what these articles say." He

had the cycle-time reduction article in the project file he carried around. To make his point, he opened up the file, took out the article, and waved it about.

Something just didn't fit. I asked to look at the article, scanning the first couple of paragraphs.

"Wait a minute," I said to Frank, "it says right here, 'cycle-time reductions are often possible with little or no *increase* in costs and they can have a huge benefit on customer service.'" The article, in other words, had never said anything about cost reduction. He had misread it, confusing time and cost, thinking that if you saved time, you would save money. So, because of this—because we had placed our "job security" above the goal—the team had spent two months on a misguided mission.

Frank grabbed the article back, scanned it, and then said, "Oh, yeah. Right."

That was it. He said nothing more. And neither did I. It was not exactly the experience of one-hundred percent success the team had wished for.

To this day, I ask myself why I said nothing.

> **The team had spent months on a misguided mission.**

But what I can see now that I didn't see then was how my response to Frank's behavior was yet another subtle example of self-betrayal. In not speaking up out of fear of what would happen if I did, I had again traded self-honoring behavior for the hope of approval and acceptance. But at the time, I wasn't clear that Frank's behavior had crossed a line by treating me and the team in a way that was not okay. I wasn't clear because I hadn't yet made it safe inside myself to feel the hurt and anger. I betrayed myself by not honoring my internal experience. And I also see that I did the best I could at the time.

Not all feelings need to be expressed, of course. But when we feel violated, when we are treated in a way we consider disrespectful, some part of ourselves needs to know that we *will* speak up against it, that we will take care of ourselves by speaking up. Avoiding the pattern of betrayal—getting beyond it—is about self-trust, trusting ourselves to speak up, to ask for support or to let someone know that we're being treated in a way that is fundamentally not okay with us.

The Piper Principle states that we attract situations to ourselves that mirror our inner struggles. We do this with the unconscious purpose of trying to resolve these "wounded" issues. That is, if we have betrayed ourselves by letting someone treat us in a way that's not okay, and we say nothing about such treatment, we "invite" situations that play out our unresolved issue with betrayal as an opportunity to resolve it. We do this for as long as it takes for us to become conscious of the underlying fear or concern, the self-judgment we hold against ourselves. This process is revealed when we can be microscopically honest with ourselves and tell ourselves why we don't speak up.

These patterns, which reflect inner-outer dilemmas, have enormous implications for productivity in the workplace. What if all barriers to reaching business goals with grace and ease are mirrors of inner self-judgments? How would we work toward goals if this were the case?

When I act using the Piper Principle, my response to barriers changes. Rather than attacking the barrier as an undesirable foe, I get curious about what can be learned from it so that I can lift it. As best I can.

At the time of this project, I was not yet fully grasping the self-judgment I had been carrying: that what I had to offer might not fundamentally be worth honoring. That *I* was not fundamentally worthy of honor.

The recognition I had been seeking from others really was about self-recognition—that I was worthy of honoring my own experience, both my inner experience and my perspective on the project; that honoring a perspective has nothing to do with the "rightness" or "wrongness" of it. This recognition didn't happen immediately, but eventually I saw what I needed to see.

Weeks later I had one more meeting with Frank. He had called and asked me to see him in his office.

The meeting began with Frank expressing appreciation for all the work I'd done; he then let me know that he was getting ready to launch a second phase of the cost-reduction program. He said that he would be inviting a number of consulting companies in addition to ours to bid on the project and that certainly our experience made us a strong contender for the job. Right then I decided not to bother with a proposal.

Then he said, "You know, we'll be winding down the team and I've started looking for jobs for people. It would really help if you could give me some feedback on a couple of the team members—I would like to find roles that would be best for them. If you're not comfortable doing this, it's okay, but I think it would be helpful for everyone concerned."

I was momentarily taken in by his friendliness. Maybe he and I *could* build a relationship. Maybe he would see that I had helpful insights to offer. I felt put on the spot, uncertain about how to proceed. I momentarily placed the opportunity to demonstrate my savvy insights to Frank above loyalty, seeing so much value in my perspective that the value of my relationships to team members shrunk in comparison. Even now I so would like to reframe this encounter in a different way, to cast a different light on what happened and see it as something other than what it turned out to be—betrayal. But acknowledging what happened clearly has helped me see how powerful the wish to be seen favorably had been operating in me.

Frank seemed particularly interested in Ray, a team member who had done an excellent job facilitating buy-in with the plant. He didn't have a job in mind for Ray and mentioned a few options he was considering.

I shared my experience: Ray was very effective working side-by-side with people in the plant, gaining their trust, explaining ideas in their language: he could work through ideas with them, checking out whether those ideas would really make a difference. He handled that time-consuming process with such effectiveness that a high level of creative thinking and enthusiasm resulted on all sides. And Ray didn't make a big deal about where ideas originated, the value of which I had come to appreciate. On the opportunity for improvement side, if Ray had been more willing to make and keep specific commitments, I could see his responsibilities on the team expanding significantly.

When I left the meeting, I went back to my office and put in a call to Ray, regretting that I had given Frank any ammunition at all, concerned about how it might be used.

But by the time Ray and I connected later in the day, Ray had already met with Frank.

"Thanks a lot," Ray said.

"What do you mean?" I asked with a sinking feeling.

"Frank gave me a review. He said he doesn't know if there will be a job for me or not. He said you told him that I didn't do enough on the project and that was the basis for his decision."

Frank must have already made up his mind before talking with me about Ray. The meeting had been a set-up, a betrayal.

"Did he tell you the whole conversation?" I asked Ray, and filled him in as much as I could, apologizing for giving Frank ammunition. I didn't see that there was much else to do. It briefly occurred to me to let Frank know that the way he had used me was unacceptable, but only briefly. Why? Was I afraid of him?

I wanted out. I'd had enough of this drama, this game. It seemed like any action on my part would only complicate the situation.

And in fact our company's role in the project and the team's role had come to a close. The group had accomplished its fundamental mission. It had identified ways to get the forty percent reduction, and for that it had at least received a letter of thanks from the president. The team hadn't gone as far as it had wanted, it wasn't at all clear how many of its ideas would be implemented, but everyone was being asked to do new jobs. Even Ray, who had kept his job after all.

We had a close-out luncheon that was a true celebration. I suggested inviting Frank; we did, and he graciously accepted. It was my last ditch effort to communicate to Frank that the team and we had accomplished much that was worthy of recognition.

At the luncheon we memorialized stories, laughed, acknowledged what we had learned, and honored each other with customized paperweights inscribed with quotes that represented each person's personality and influence on the team.

A little over a year later I had lunch with an individual who had taken over much of the company's production operations. She had participated in our company's executive coaching program and our lunch was a follow-up meeting for feedback on her experience with the program.

I took the opportunity to ask about what had changed in operations at the company recently, and she mentioned several innovations that I recognized as the team's recommendations. The company had even gone for the radical redesign of the manufacturing process. "Frank's done a lot," she said. "It was a good move to bring him in." I realized with some disappointment that she, and no doubt others, had not linked the changes on any level to the team's work.

Our victory felt hollow. Knowing that change had been achieved was overshadowed by the lack of recognition the team had received. I had, nonetheless, learned something about betrayal and fixation on results without consideration of relationships. I had always delighted in my results-driven orientation, but because of this experience, I had become more conscious of the fact that other aspects of an experience mattered too. It had been difficult learning, but I saw how balancing relationships and results could increase productivity. I committed myself to learning more fully how to do this and our consulting practice changed substantially because of it.

The team got together for dinner several years after the project concluded for a re-celebration. People spoke about how their careers had evolved and how being on the team had made such a difference for them personally. These testimonials were gratifying to hear. There was also resignation that although most of the team's recommendations had been implemented, no one on the team felt that their contributions had been acknowledged by anyone outside of the team. The team acknowledged that no doubt the ideas had been implemented because manufacturing had adopted them as their own. I personally felt that I had let the team down by not supporting them differently, wishing that they had experienced a win on all levels. It was disappointing.

Recognition. Betrayal. Recognition. Betrayal.

I was in a double-bind. Wrong to want recognition. Bad if I didn't get it. Betraying myself by wishing the experience to be different than it is. This is a hard place to be.

In coaching myself and others on this issue, I have slowly come to understand that feeling worthy of recognition is something independent from receiving recognition. When I feel worthy of recognition I am detached from whether it happens. This sense of worth can be attained independent of particular events, how projects turn out, or what results are accomplished. As I grasp this, I see also the value of recognition: it feels affirming and encouraging to be acknowledged. I find it easier now to notice the contributions others make and that I make. All contributions are valued. Recognition on this level is rooted in gratitude.

I am grateful for everything that has allowed this awareness to evolve, including the lack of recognition from Frank and others that created the opportunity and motivation to reach this place of productive peace. I recognize the value in what has unfolded. I can let go of wishing it had been different.

> **When I feel worthy of recognition, I am detached from whether it happens.**

And I can also see that more learning is possible.

We have started a new project recently, one that challenges me because I want to play a supportive role rather than the leadership role I might typically play. This change is necessary because the demands on my time are increasing and because it will expand the leadership opportunity for others. However, this "on the sidelines" role is not natural for me. At the same time, I have quickly discovered that there is much freedom in this new role. It provides the opportunity to stand back, observe more, see the big picture, and appreciate the contributions others make.

At our first project meeting, I found myself wondering whether others valued me in this new role. I was aware of how challenged I felt, how hard I was working to develop new "step-back" skills. I heard myself make a couple of digs at the ideas others offered as if to say, "Hey, don't you see what I know?" I winced as I did it and then did it again. But shortly thereafter, I was able to recognize and acknowledge the sadness and hurt I felt in "perceiving" I was not being valued. I was then able to value myself and feel grate-

ful for this experience and for what I was learning.

I also saw that it would be fine for me to just ask the team for the support: Tell me what you appreciate about what I am doing in this new role. In considering how I could just simply say this, I immediately begin to more fully consider what I appreciate about the expanded roles others were playing and what we can achieve together. Telling the truth to others and myself is a much more respectful, honoring approach, and is helping me stay productive in this new role.

How wonderful is the release of preoccupied energy,

> **I set an intention going forward to reach goals with ever more grace and ease.**

letting go of fears about the value of my contribution! It allows me to participate fully so that I stay productive and so do others—I acknowledge more and "make digs" less. Seeing this, experiencing gratitude for learning, is energizing.

I set an intention going forward to see and address ever more quickly these opportunities for accelerating productivity—for learning how to reach goals with ever more grace and ease.

Balking Heads

Will I Be Blaming or Learning Today?

▼

When so rich a harvest
is before us,
why do we not gather it?
All is in our hands
if we will but use it.

—

ELIZABETH SETON

Balking Heads

ON the job, having responsibility often means possessing the authority to act with only minimal guidance. But authority and responsibility aren't always aligned. Sometimes we are given a job to do, held responsible for doing it, but don't feel we have the authority to make the decisions that are necessary to complete the work successfully. Taking authority over ourselves in this situation means that we take responsibility to address the situation *itself.*

For example, one of our clients was responsible for shepherding seven global teams through a complex research process. He was responsible for seeing that all seven teams delivered high quality research results on time. But when we began working for this individual, it became clear that he did not have the authority to hire the leaders of these teams. The who-to-hire authority was held by his boss's boss. Moreover, when he suggested candidates for new team leaders, and they were turned down, he was not given "data" about how the candidate's qualifications had not matched with job specifications. And the time that it consequently took to fill open positions was jeopardizing his ability to deliver results on time. Giving senior man-

agement feedback that it was not productive for this job-
hiring-guessing-game to go on was difficult because direct
feedback was not the norm in this organi-

> **Giving feedback was not the norm.**

zation. However, our client took responsibility to learn the skills for delivering feedback even in this challenging situation.

Another company, also a client, struggled to define job responsibilities for years.
No matter to whom I talked in this organization—whether
from production, marketing, research and development, or
human resources—discussions about work almost always
led to a core frustration: job roles and responsibilities were
not clearly defined. What they meant was "I can't do my job
because I haven't been given clear authority to do it."

This nearly single-minded focus on roles and responsibilities, and the attachment people showed to getting
clear about them, puzzled me at first. Often employees
seemed more interested in talking about the scope of their
jobs than actually doing them.

Over time, I came to appreciate how employee preoc-
cupation with responsibility—how much or how little was
given or taken away—reflected the way the organization
gave feedback about how an employee was doing. Being
given additional responsibility "told" an individual that he
or she was performing well on the job. Having responsibility removed meant the opposite—and produced fear.
Fear of this type existed because employees were not given
direct feedback about their work or appropriate coaching
to make course-correction realistic.

People often avoid giving and receiving course-corrective feedback because it can be delivered in a way that

implies someone is doing something wrong. This creates a "negative" experience for all concerned. Being attacked, the receiver feels compelled to "defend" and, as a result, the deliverer of feedback feels unheard.

Such an approach reflects a "right-wrong" model, which most businesses follow. That model maintains that there's a right and wrong way to execute job responsibilities, with a boss who usually sits in judgment of performance. These authorities have firm opinions about employees, but the individuals who work for them often don't know what they are or how well they're doing. I've heard employees at many companies describe their experiences of leaving a meeting with senior management. They receive no specific feedback, but are left feeling that it didn't go well and fearing that their careers are over. And, based upon the quick judgments senior management can often make about people in their organizations, their intuitions are often dead-on.

When I am working with an organization like this, where effective feedback skills are not in place at high lev-

els of the organization, and this "withholding feedback" culture cascades through the organization, I know change will be challenging. I am probably dealing with a CEO who is not okay with learning—with receiving feedback about what they could do differently to accelerate productivity in their organizations. I know what this is like—for a long time I resisted receiving feedback like this myself.

In the enlightened company, a learning model is in place in which productivity accelerates and the concepts of responsibility and feedback also shift dramatically. Feedback is welcomed because the feedback process is trusted. Everyone supports the idea that employees are doing the best they can moment by moment. Individuals constantly look at those moment by moment choices, see what can be learned, and consider how to apply what they've learned going forward. They take responsibility for getting the feedback they need to do their jobs well and address whatever makes doing their job hard. They note what consumes more resources than need be, adds time, adds stress, or lowers creativity and enthusiasm; and they surface this information so that it can be addressed. In other words, everyone learns how to reach goals more productively.

In the learning model there are no mistakes or failures, only successes and learning opportunities. And since almost anything can be done with greater grace and ease, there is only learning. But such learning can only happen if we see our responses and actions as choices. When our responses are made automatically, when we operate on automatic pilot, there is no choice involved and hence no learning available. Having a learning orientation requires us to assume responsibility for the situations we create based on the many, many choices we make throughout the day. The goal isn't about making right choices, but learning whether the choices we make are working for us or not—and if not, to experiment with other choices, to have ever more conscious awareness of what we do, and thus take even greater responsibility for our situation.

When I'm with people who don't see responsibility this way—who assume little authority over themselves and hence over the situations they find themselves in, who want to blame others for situations they're in and refuse to look for the learning in a situation—I feel as if I'm surrounded by balking heads: talk, talk, talk, resist, resist, resist is all they do. These encounters can feel draining, unproductive, and unrewarding.

Before I could learn how to address this type of situation effectively, however, I had to confront my own resistance to learning about resistance. I had to stop making resistance wrong, and start seeing the learning opportunity that resistance offers.

‡ ‡ ‡

Early in my career I had the opportunity to lead a discussion among key account managers from a successful pharmaceutical company. This newly formed group was charged with responding to requests from the company's most important customers—these requests generally involving customizing products or services to better meet the customer's needs.

Before their department was formed, marketing had

been organized entirely around products. This required customers, such as a hospital network or a managed care organization, to traverse many company departments to set up the customized products and services they required.

Significant questions were on the table: How should the company's internal processes be changed to respond to requests for customized products and services? What level of commitment to customization did the company actually have? What level of customization was appropriate given the dynamics of a rapidly changing marketplace? How much authority did the group have to make promises to customers?

The new group had been in place for over a year and some strides had been made in improving company relationships with several important customers, but these key strategic issues hadn't been addressed. Consequently there was still ambiguity about the organization's commitment to becoming customer-focused. The new customer marketing department knew that there were people in the company already building a case for their undoing.

For the first hour of the meeting the discussion was stilted, the atmosphere thick with unspoken communication—averted glances, sudden shoulder drooping, lack of energy. The group struggled to set a direction for the day without enthusiasm.

What was going on? Clearly the difficulty the group was having deciding on an approach for the day mirrored the struggle over what the group thought it could accomplish in general. On the one hand, there was support for an unfettered exploration of the group's role and responsibilities, to investigate the possibility of spearheading a broad-based company shift to a customer-driven organization. On the other hand, there was a pull to constrain the discussion to ideas the members knew were the most politically viable and would incur the least company resistance.

The company thought about revenue growth in ways that were traditional for the industry—by promoting brands, not by building relationships with large customers and focusing on their needs. So some in the group wanted to remain realistic about what was possible, which meant not setting themselves up for failure by getting caught in radical thinking, or proposing a charter that would meet with too much organizational resistance.

I've noticed that the way a group approaches a specific problem often indicates how the group works together generally. If a group is having trouble figuring out a focus for the day, as this group was, then it is probably having trouble with focus in general. This isn't surprising—what limits a group generally will limit it in specific situations. Groups and individuals who are conscious of the way they work are better able to course-correct and accelerate their productivity. They can step back to consider how they work and identify what is required to move to a higher level of effectiveness. Whether a group can see the relationship between its approach to problem solving and itself as a body reflects its level of awareness; when that level is high, the group observes its own effectiveness consciously, and frequently experiments with alternative approaches to arrive at innovative solutions. When awareness is low, a group tends to operate on automatic pilot and to blame outsiders or one another for ineffectiveness. Simply becoming aware of when the group is or isn't being effective, and experimenting with new ways to work, the group—and by extension the corporation—gains a huge opportunity to improve productivity. I find that individuals are often clear about what someone else can do to enhance their productivity, but are seldom deft in shifting this examination to themselves. (This was also true of me when I was working with this client.)

The difficulty the group had in charting a direction for itself also reflected a lack of leadership, which limited its effectiveness generally. There was no official group head, just an acting head whose role was compromised because the company had been recruiting for her position for some time.

Moreover, the person who had called the meeting in

hopes of encouraging the group to clarify the role of the new department, wasn't (as it probably should have been) the acting head, but a department member. Seeing that a lack of leadership was holding the group back, this organizer went to everyone in the department advocating the need to establish its direction, role, and responsibilities. Once that was done, the organizer maintained, the group could proactively seek endorsement of its views from management.

The only one who had opposed this meeting was the acting head, who felt that calling for it implied that she wasn't providing sufficient leadership. But under the pressure of everyone else being in favor, the acting head agreed to the meeting. Enthusiastic for the opportunity to practice my facilitating skills, shielded by pride, I went along, confident that once everyone was in the room, I would help get the job done.

> **Enthusiastic for the opportunity, shielded by pride, I went along.**

As the meeting got underway, it became clear that the issue on the minds of everyone present (including me) was how cooperative the acting head would be. We all wondered whether she had come to the meeting to participate openly or to prove the meeting wasn't a good idea in the first place.

It is often true that when a shared goal isn't present within a group, a common enemy will emerge. Although I didn't see it at the time, I had climbed aboard a train of consensus that the acting head was enemy number one.

Because it was her idea to meet, the organizer was committed to the position that the meeting would help ensure the department's success. The acting head, who felt she had been forced into the meeting, was committed to the position that the meeting wasn't a good idea. And so we had the dance of the balking heads—the acting head talked all around her frustration and hurt about how the meeting had come about through a kind of mutiny, effectively preventing creative discussion about the topic the meeting was called to address. People resist, or balk, when they have a position that is not being heard and don't trust that it can be heard. Balking is a "useful" strategy for gaining the illusion of control. By talking in circles, restating positions, offering confusing information, she was thwarting action (the development of a strategy) with which she didn't agree.

> Resistance, I thought, was the enemy; it was wrong. It didn't occur to me to consider that I was resisting.

From my perspective at the time, as a results-oriented achiever, the only useful participation I could see was participation that moved us toward the goal. Resistance, I thought, was the enemy; it was wrong. It didn't occur to me to consider that I was resisting. The fact that we were having trouble getting the meeting off the ground was about the group's resistance, I felt, especially the resistance of the acting head; I was blind to mine, which took the form of me telling myself that the dispute between the acting head and the organizer was preventing me from assisting the group to realize its objectives—and preventing me from being successful.

My attitude deserved resistance from the group, which it duly received. This led to my strong-arming my way among the group members, asking pressing questions, and cutting off discussion when it seemed designed to stonewall the day. I shamed the nervous ones into participating, and at last, struggling, pushed the group to deliver a summary of its thinking on the issues. I got a result, all right, but at the expense of my relationship with some group members. Entirely unconscious of what had happened, I resolved never to facilitate another discussion unless I had met individually with each person first to check on their willingness to participate.

I was learning, I told myself consolingly. What I didn't see and what was crucial to an understanding of how I had created distance between myself and the group, was the source of my own resistance: my nervousness about my own possible failure. Because of this I had become controlling to achieve the task for which I had been given responsibility. Instead of sharing creativity, enthu-

siasm and inspiration, which would have made achieving a better result in less time more likely, we shared an arduous time.

Reflecting on this experience later, I gave myself a hard time for not seeing my own resistance to what was taking place. But I now realize that my resistance served a purpose. We have to protect the fragile parts of ourselves that we characterize as lacking, inadequate, or unworthy until we're ready to see what we need to see to experience the truth about ourselves. The outside layers of misperception have to be peeled away to reach the inner core of personal truth.

The journey to more conscious awareness and greater effectiveness can take time—it takes as long as it does—but it has many rewards. One of them, for me, has been a greater respect for other people's resistance. The more I've gotten in touch with the parts of my emotional self I've protected, the more respect I have for the resistance in others. The resistance serves as a shield against this tender area.

Ultimately, the meeting of key account managers had some success. A summary I prepared of the group's thinking on roles and responsibilities had an impact: it prompted senior management to debate the role of the department directly. Management set time aside to formally clarify the company's commitment to a customer focus; they outlined the roles and responsibilities for the department, and finally hired a department head. My ability to mow down resistance to get to a result had given me a degree of positive appeal with some in the organization and I was asked to facilitate the discussion among senior management.

Because the company approached decisions in a hierarchical fashion, individuals on upper and lower steps of the managerial ladder were often not in the same room when significant debate occurred. It was thought that upper management wouldn't or couldn't speak candidly in the presence of lower management and vice versa.

Once the debate with senior management started, I understood fully why this was so. Upper management generally had little confidence in their reports—in this case, the new department—and this lack of trust steered its thinking on the definition of roles and responsibilities. Because upper management didn't want to risk "confrontation," direct feedback to the department seemed out of the realm of possibility; instead, upper management took the cheerleading approach, promising to support the department. Senior management thought this pledge would inspire the customer-focused department to increase performance. But the responsibility for ensuring this improvement was placed squarely on the shoulders of the new department head—who wasn't present and would therefore hear of his "assignment" second hand. In other words, senior management wanted improvement but didn't want to be honest with the very people it made responsible for achieving it.

They're shirking their responsibility for the group's success, I thought to myself, and by extension, the success of the company's reorientation to greater customer focus. There's no way their plan will get the department on track without a lot more false starts and bumps in the road, I decided. As my thinking unfolded, I piled on the evidence. They can't see the issue that needs addressing because they are looking in the wrong direction. When people don't see what they need to see, when they don't say what needs to be said, they find themselves becoming balking heads. Their energy is not focused in a particularly productive direction.

I tried to feel better about the situation by reminding myself that, at least among themselves, upper management had felt free to express its frustration with the department. Management had trusted me enough to be open in front of me, and I had given it direct input on

their responsibility in the situation—how departments can flounder without direction and support from management. Wasn't that progress?

It would be best, I concluded, not to challenge upper management too much and jeopardize what progress had been made. I was experimenting with not pushing as hard and as fast as I had done earlier in my career. Ease up, I told myself.

Experimenting with new behaviors is helpful. However, my experimentation still carried the implicit expectation that I do it right. And this mirrored my expectation that senior management do it right.

What I didn't see at the time was that upper management didn't have the skills to handle the situation any more effectively than they had. If they had had more effective skills in that moment, they would have handled it differently. For what they knew about themselves, for how they understood their role, for the level of communication skills they possessed, they had done the best they could. However, for their "failing" I had, unconsciously, judged them wrong. The recognition of this judgment would have revealed my own blind spot about condemning myself when I didn't possess skills I thought I should have, and perhaps would have allowed me to address the issue more productively.

> **They can't see the issue that needs addressing because they are looking in the wrong direction.**

By way of trying to let myself off the hook for not confronting the group, I told myself to honor the pace at which people proceed to break down the walls that limit their effectiveness. In doing so, I was beginning to honor my own pace.

The group never achieved its mission—it continued to flounder. Without leadership and a true sense of purpose, without getting the necessary feedback, it could only make a half-hearted effort. And in spite of substantial skills in customizing services for customers, the company has continued to be ambivalent about the shift to a customer focus.

As I consider this, part of me still wants to make what happened and myself wrong. The voice of my inner critic frets, "I should have been able to help them address this situation more effectively." However, what I am learning is that when I hold the expectation that I could have done better than I did, I am being inaccurate. The truth is that I did the best I could at the time. I have no way of knowing what would have happened if I had approached the situation differently. But I do know that partially as a result of the way the situation unfolded, compassion for myself has deepened. And that makes me more effective in raising opportunities for learning, and for that I'm grateful.

> **The truth is that I did the best I could at the time.**

‡ ‡ ‡

Several years later, I was asked to facilitate a two-day meeting between members of a team responsible for rolling out a "hot product," one that was projected to generate a billion dollars in revenue within three years. The head of the launch team explained to me that he had been struggling to lead its members who, he felt, had bypassed him on critical decisions. He had found himself frequently embarrassed when top management had asked him to justify a decision on which he hadn't been briefed.

Also, others had told him that they had had difficulty communicating with the launch team—its members didn't seem willing to accept input from anyone about their approach or plans. This situation had made top management nervous about whether the critical new product rollout would be effective.

When I met with the team members individually before the meeting, I had an awkward experience. Almost all of them saw no reason for a meeting. At least one thought he should be running the meeting rather than me. Others thought they'd be too busy to attend, while the remainder were annoyed by management's position that it was possible to improve the team's functioning at all because, they indicated, you couldn't improve on perfection. Conducting these interviews, I had the sense of what it would be like to interrogate hostile witnesses. If the team members weren't clear on the value of the meeting, then it was more than likely that nothing productive would come of it. The silent message I was getting from the team members was, "The meeting is a dumb idea and a big waste of time!"

At the time the department head and I had just completed a highly successful three-day gathering with his peers. The people involved in that meeting had expressed confusion and resistance at its onset, but by the end there was strong alignment with a plan for the upcoming year and wild enthusiasm for what had occurred at the meeting. Buoyed by this experience, he and I brushed aside concerns about the "hot team" meeting and forged ahead. And hit a wall—the organized resistance of the team.

While the department head's peers had initially been resistant in their meeting, they were not an established team; they were, therefore, ill-prepared to mount a resistance, should they have wanted to, in an organized fashion. The hot team, on the other hand, had become highly sophisticated about confronting authority. They thrived on doing so.

The first act of the hot team's resistance took the form of an encounter over chair arrangement. This confrontation escalated quickly, the group immediately rallied to defend the person who had challenged the chair arrangement, I waffled on the issue, and the team leader disappeared into his own head. We never quite recovered.

Though I was trembling, I made an attempt to get the group to see how it banded together when someone from the outside made a suggestion the group didn't like. I wanted to show them how they resisted input from others. I invited them to consider these patterns in the context of how they

might affect their ability to create a successful product launch. But these patterns represented group blind spots that required more trust to discuss openly than I had established with the group at that juncture. The group had made its point that the gathering wasn't a good idea in the first place, and was subsequently reluctant to jeopardize the opportunity to be right.

We got to the end of the meeting with some modest plans to take action in several areas of concern—nothing like the quantum leap the team leader and I had hoped for. The team had indeed "proved" that they were right about the meeting's "worthlessness." I licked my wounds and "went for the learning" about how rigid and controlling I could get when I get a whiff of mob mentality. And I definitely recognized the unpleasantness of the experience.

I started thinking about what I might need to learn to be more effective and productive in situations like this. Before we can recognize an aspect of ourselves for which we judge ourselves harshly yet cannot acknowledge, we can experience involvement with an issue repeatedly in the form of situations that don't work out. These patterns are a form of feedback to ourselves. This is why, for example, we may find ourselves continually attracted to the "wrong" kind of boss or client. It's our attempt to address and resolve the underlying issue that such a relationship represents. In my case, the issue involved plunging ahead with individuals who were resisting my approach to leading them in discussion.

> The hot team had become highly sophisticated about confronting authority. They thrived on doing so.

Words from my past came back to me:

"They are keeping me from doing a good job!"

And I saw that I had been blaming the group for the meeting's failure. Using the Piper Principle, which I had become aware of and used more and more frequently, I realized that this indicated something in me that I didn't want to see, that I was resisting learning.

Balking heads indeed!

But what was I resisting? What if my lack of skill at handling resistance was keeping me from doing a good job? What would I need to learn so meetings like the one I'd just experienced could be handled with grace and ease and its participants treated with respect and compassion?

Because of my pride and self-assurance, which had on other occasions enabled me to take on significant challenges, it was tough to consider that I had significantly more to learn about facilitation. I didn't want that to be the case. To accept and recognize this, to know I still had lots to learn, was physically uncomfortable. I felt vulnerable recognizing this. Leading a group was one thing—leading a group fully aware that I could, and probably would make mistakes because I had much to learn—was quite another. It's far easier to blame others and focus on their mistakes. But I couldn't deny the truth—I did have much to learn. And I discovered there was relief in that recognition, in admitting it to myself. Not needing to be perfect. Not needing to control things so they came out "right." Just doing my best and being willing to learn.

> **I had begun to understand that individuals feel resistant when they don't feel heard, or they fear the consequences of the direction a situation is heading.**

There was something deeper to consider, too. I had been blaming others for their resistance, making resistance the enemy. What if resistance had value in itself? What purpose might resistance be serving? Perhaps my ineffectiveness in dealing with the team's resistance had to do with making resistance itself wrong. Resistance could be a good thing—resistance to viral infection is good. If I was going to stop judging others harshly for their resistance, maybe I needed to stop judging myself for mine.

I had begun to understand that individuals feel resistant when they don't feel heard, or they fear the consequences of the direction a situation is heading. Resistance is also evidence of not listening—when I am resisting a position, I am not asking questions, not exploring what is being offered. I didn't have this piece of the equation figured out entirely, but I felt I had made a good start. I was learning, I told myself. And I experienced the deep truth of that statement.

My new attitude about resistance and insights came too late to benefit the hot team, I told myself at the time, subtly still resisting what had unfolded, making it wrong. Things at the company turned out disappointingly. The team leader lost his job some months later, and the new product was pulled from the market a few months after launch for reasons others had known about but had been

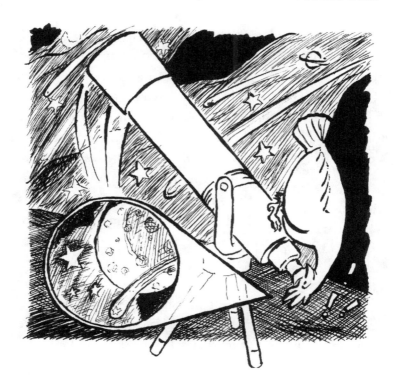

unable to get the team's attention to address. Faced with drastically lower projections in revenue, the company was forced to downsize dramatically.

Seeing all this motivated me—if I had had the skill to work effectively with the group, the result, with its potential for positive impact, could have been staggering. I recommitted myself to discovering what the purpose of resistance was—what value it served—and to developing my skills at handling resistance effectively. I was no longer blaming myself for what had happened, but encouraging myself to learn.

And slowly I came to see a great deal of value in resistance. Resistance was evidence that positions were being taken that considered only part of the story—resistance was an invitation to consider how to raise myself and others above individual positions, to see the bigger picture. This would require valuing positions, not dismissing them. I was starting to understand resistance at a deeper level, deeper than simply seeing it as a tug-of-political-war between two positions. Resistance, I could see, was really an invitation to creativity—an invitation to consider a perspective, a more creative solution, than either of the two separate positions offered. In fact the energy of resistance was powerful and could be used to elevate the thinking—raise it to that higher perspective.

> **Individuals who express resistance are demonstrating fear, and that takes trust to address.**

But resistance was not just about results, it was also about relationships. Individuals who express resistance are demonstrating fear, and that takes trust to address. We

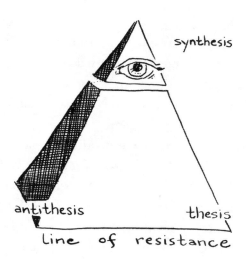

protect what appears fragile and is valuable to us.
Resistance would be a sign, I told myself, that I have yet
to fully appreciate the full value in someone or something.
Resistance would be the cue that I could make a situation
safer.

Understanding all of this has brought both gentleness
and passion to my work and improved the quality of the
work I do.

‡ ‡ ‡

Some years later my partner and I were working
with an organization that was taking steps to implement
employee performance measurements, to track how
everyday decisions impacted financial performance. The
organization had been successful at establishing some
measures to increase fiscal performance, but needed
additional information.

My partner and I worked with the company to identify the measures that would be appropriate and then assisted them in modifying their internal systems so that performance data could be captured and reported in a meaningful fashion. Early in the assignment, we talked about needing to educate management about using the new data. We also discussed how individuals could be motivated to perform better by goal-attainment or by fear ("the carrot or stick"). If the new measurements were used to reveal performance errors, then employees might respond defensively, become involved in trying to justify the data. Employee interest in why the results were what they were—desirable if real change was to be made—would then be stifled in the rush to self-justification.

Once management had the data, it could proceed in one of two ways. It could support employees in setting meaningful targets, asking them what would be needed to meet a given target. This would set up one environment. Or it could pounce on the new data looking for problems and trying to identify who was "screwing up." That would set up quite another.

We explained this distinction to those most closely involved in the project, and they seemed to understand. They said they could relate to what we were saying about "beating people up with numbers." Some of them said they had experienced just such events personally. But ultimately, they reasoned that their responsibilities lay elsewhere. Their job was to get the numbers, they maintained, not to figure out how the numbers should be used. This part of the equation was fuzzy to them, not so important. Not clearly valuable.

I felt myself getting annoyed at their resistance, at their unwillingness to see something that I considered key to the project's success. I was annoyed at my inability to express the point effectively. But I remembered that I can be resistant when I'm unwilling to learn or see value in another approach or view. Rather than get hung up about their resistance, I decided to relax and watch what unfolded with open curiosity.

The new data was generated. When management met to discuss it, the reaction was as predicted—they pounced. "Why do we have so many products that are bringing in so little revenue?" one manager asked. "Look at this business unit over here," someone else added, "they're really out of line!" The senior financial officer, who was also attending the meeting, shook his head in a discouraged fashion, and I saw others in the room exchange worried looks. I could see how the discussion would go.

I took the project manager aside and pointed out that the issue we had discussed about the constructive use of the data was now rearing its head. "Buy-in and employee enthusiasm for change is going to go south in a hurry," I told him, "if the numbers are used against people, to find fault. People will use that experience as evidence that it's not safe to have 'bad numbers'. They will spend more time constructing explanations about the data than honestly considering the data and gaining insights from it. Instead of using data to accelerate progress toward improvements, we'll simply use the data to explain what we already have, thereby reproducing what we have."

He looked at me and shook his head. "I hear what you're saying," he said, "but we're not a touchy-feely com-

EVIDENCE   *Balking*   MORE EVIDENCE
                  DEFENSIVE BEHAVIOR

pany. People around here are used to being called on the carpet to get change to happen. That's the way it's done around here."

I suggested he participate in a program we offer, our executive coaching sessions, to explore how he could effectively raise issues with upper management about their response to the data. I told him our coaching program would identify how he could lead in this area and enhance his effectiveness in shepherding change in his organization.

No way was he going near that one! He related a personal experience about receiving negative feedback from associates who had gathered just for that purpose. I could see that it had been painful for him and suddenly, I could appreciate his resistance to coaching and feedback. I could see that resistance sometimes serves a useful function, when people feel they're about to be overwhelmed, for example, with the "brutal truth." If I had had a painful experience like his, I wouldn't want to revisit it either. I could see that what I called resistance was for this executive a shield that had been necessary for survival. He was the best judge of when it would be safe enough for it to be removed, not I. Patience and acceptance were the tools I needed, not a bulldozer. It was challenging to wed this new understanding with my old desire to plow through obstacles like another's resistance. My desire was to achieve success. The drive to understand and the drive to succeed were seemingly in conflict.

> **They will spend more time constructing explanations to explain the data than honestly considering it.**

I thought about the times I had used the bulldozer approach to plow through the resistance of others, disregarding the messages I was being given by them in such situations. I realized I could be more patient with others and allow things to unfold at their own pace.

The project team continued to work on getting the company the data it required. Whenever my partner and I saw fear and concern arise over the numbers, we tried to address those feelings in a gentle way. In one case, for example, a manager received data summaries from us about her unit and rapidly flipped through them, saying under her breath, "Whew, no screw-ups here...great, no screw-ups there!" Her immediate focus revealed her involvement with blame, with a right-wrong model, and I talked to her about her feelings one-on-one.

Later, several individuals had a chance to show the reports for their units to their peers. We encouragingly told them to talk about what they were learning from the reports. But many hadn't learned much. What they had done was construct intricate explanations for why the

> "I'm not sure I really see the difference between using the data for defending versus using it for learning."

numbers were what they were. In one case, a product for a key customer was available only twenty percent of the time. The person in charge of explaining that result dutifully reported why that was so, rather than realizing that, hey, that wasn't going to work and, instead, exploring what might be done to change the situation. As I looked around the room I realized that many people did not recognize their own defensiveness because in that situation, it was the only response they knew.

Some months later we gathered again. This time there were some important wins to report. Several individuals had found creative ways for using the data to create positive results.

For example, the people in one unit had realized that though the processing cost they were assessing per order was constant, the size of the orders varied widely. Those responsible for the unit made a decision to implement a change—they made the order-processing cost dependent on order size—and the financial impact of this change was equivalent to the cost of the entire program we were conducting several times over. I was happy to see that this unit and some of the others were using the numbers in innovative ways.

Other units, however, didn't exercise much creativity or experimentation—I saw "defending" on their part rather than learning. We again gently raised the point about a learning versus a defending response in relation to performance-against-data issues.

One of the "defenders" raised his hand. "Could you talk a little more about that?" he asked hesitantly. "I'm not sure I really see the difference between using the data for defending versus learning."

I was stunned at what this question implied—that I had made many inaccurate assumptions about what concepts people "should" be able to take in. We spoke again, slowing the pace, bringing in a softer, easier energy. "It's about what you tell yourself when you look at the data," we said. "Are your thoughts, like, 'This is bad, really bad and I'm going to get called on the carpet to explain?' If those were my thoughts, I would be concerned about being judged a poor manager. I might research factors to explain the data away, so the numbers would seem reasonable. If, on the other hand, I had a learning attitude, I would more likely think, 'How come we're at that level? What's going on?' I would see the situation as a chance to learn something that I didn't know. Hopefully, that insight would enable me to help change the results."

The group was listening carefully, as I wasn't attacking them but revealing something about me. "To take the learning path," I continued, "I'd have to be *willing* to be judged a poor manager. I'd have to be *willing* to risk experiencing the thing I would rather protect myself from going through."

I had seen this operating in my own case when I had struggled to accept I was still a facilitator-in-training, and always would be. I shared with the group how hard this had been for me at first since I generally preferred to be perceived as perfectly competent all the time, and we laughed easily over my unrealistic expectation.

Another defender spoke up. "Well, maybe there's something we could be doing that we're not," she said, "something we could be learning."

"I'll tell you what," she said to us, "why don't you come down to our office for a day and let's look over the numbers together. You can help me see what there is to learn from them that I'm not seeing. You can show me if there's something we could be doing to plan production differently."

It was an exceptional invitation and represented an opening to explore a learning attitude. It represented a major shift in approach, a less defensive posture, that could lead to greater productivity. I realized that at least one manager had found her own path to considering a learning orientation—and that this shift possibly couldn't have been reached by pushing and shoving her. I recognized again the value of allowing things to unfold at their own pace as a way to address resistance, balking and blocking. I recognized that while I may think I know what timing is best, I may not know. And I recognized the value of being able to share honestly and openly my own learning process—that owning my learning process makes it safer for others to own theirs.

This learning about the value of sharing my own

process ultimately started me down a path that led to this book. So what I initially identified as a wrong path—that I had wanted to leap in and control and get back on course because I "knew best"—turned out to be a fruitful path indeed.

I could also see that I wanted the group to take action in a way that I had not been willing to do myself. I had wanted them to challenge senior management's right-wrong attitude regarding performance data. At the onset of the project, I had briefly broached the need to address with senior management how the data would be used, but I hadn't pursued this idea because it hadn't been received well and I didn't want to jeopardize the project. I saw that there was an opportunity to be both stronger and gentler in offering advice on strategy at the outset of a project. I saw that there was another level of learning to go to—how to deal effectively with resistance. I also saw that there was no way to know what would have happened if I had acted differently. It was all about learning.

I can now see that resistance is an invitation to discover something new, something that couldn't have been seen otherwise. Resistance is a signal that it's time to pay close attention because some important learning is at hand.

I've been more gentle with myself since I've discovered how I have resisted learning in the past. When I find myself playing the right-wrong game, wanting projects to go "perfectly", to go the way I think they should go, I stop and make it okay for me to be learning. I invite myself to consider a perspective where all views are valid. With more compassion for myself and greater acceptance of the pace at which I'm learning, I experience deeper compassion for

others as well. And what flows from the invitation for greater creativity often brings a smile.

Joining THE AAA Club

Appreciating Aggravating Agitators

▼

We waste our substance
and dampen our spirits
by insisting on seeing our shadows
as negative, rarely looking at the trapped
energy that they contain.

—

Jean Houston

Joining THE AAA Club

FOR a long while I believed that if aggravation was present in a relationship, someone else was doing something wrong. When I felt aggravated, I presumed someone was trying to make my life more difficult, which was wrong of them to do. I would feel irritated and upset about this, and I would think, 'Why can't they understand how hard they are making me work! If they keep it up, the whole effort is going to come out badly!' In so many words, I'd let them know 'You're doing something wrong—stop it,' and I'd put distance between myself and others in this process.

On the other hand, when I experienced other people's aggravation, I often concluded they were being excessively emotional. They were jumping to conclusions or behaving irrationally. But since it didn't seem safe to communicate this, I would typically change directions, silently separating from them.

It took me some time to see aggravation for what it is—an opportunity to understand myself and others and get closer to them in the process. But before that could happen, I had to learn to see the way that escaping from aggravating agitators mirrored my attempts to escape from my own feelings.

Aggravating situations can come in all sizes—small annoyances to big problems. A number of years ago I watched myself aggravate a CEO who, in my opinion, got upset for show. This resulted in my literally being thrown off a train. The train was standing still, so my speedy exit didn't qualify as a catastrophe; nevertheless, the incident came early in my career and helped form my initial strategy in dealing with aggravating agitators.

I was employed by a Midwestern railroad as a market manager—a liaison between railroad operations and grain suppliers—and found myself in the middle of Oklahoma winter-wheat territory in a business car loaded with grain shippers, the CEO, and his administrative aide. A business car is a railroad car that has been converted into an entertainment lounge; most shippers really liked the idea of being asked aboard one for an evening of drinking, dining, and informal kibitzing. I was less than two years out of college, new to the position of market manager, and a novice at the fine skill of entertaining customers.

In those days, the late '70s, the railroad industry wasn't yet deregulated, and railroad business customers weren't so much appreciated as tolerated. (Deregulation has changed a lot, but according to shippers I know, it hasn't totally changed the attitude railroads sometimes have about their customers.) Midwest railroads have tracks that lead from farm elevators to markets, and in those days, railroads pretty much called the shots about empty shipping-car availability and frequency of service. In railroad meetings I attended, the prevailing attitude was that rail-

roading would be a lot more fun if we didn't have the shippers and their complaints.

The railroad had petitioned for bankruptcy and was in
the process of filing a formal reorganization plan with the
court. So the president needed the shippers to appeal to
the court in favor of allowing the company to continue
operations. The president especially needed support from
the big grain shippers—they had political pull in
Washington—so he was focused on ways to win their alle-
giance.

The grain elevator owners, who were also the shippers,
had felt for years that the railroad was insensitive to their
needs—recurrent car shortages had, for example, hurt
them badly. In light of this, and hoping to trade their support for more attention, the shippers had gotten together
months earlier and approached the railroad president with
a unique proposal: send us one of your employees for three
months, we'll teach them the grain business, and then
we'll have someone at your company who understands
what we're up against. My shoulder was tapped for this
dubious honor and I was sent off to Iowa, an important
grain-production state.

True to their word, the grain shippers introduced me
to their business. They showed me how they traded
futures to protect against price fluctuations; negotiated
contracts with corn processing plants; loaded a one-hun-
dred-hopper car train and then transferred it to an ocean
vessel a thousand miles away; and managed the flow of
dozens of farm wagons dropping off each day's harvest. It
was clear that the railroad's pricing structure and car allo-
cation system had seriously complicated the shippers' lives

and made it more difficult for them to respond to market dynamics in the global trade environment in which they operated.

So there I was in the railroad car on the heels of my return from education with the shippers. They were particularly upset by a new railway pricing structure that had been introduced a month earlier. It would force their grain to travel all the way to Gulf Coast ports by rail, thus denying them the option of storage and transloading (moving grain off rail cars and onto trucks or barges) along the Mississippi for local use or, if market dynamics changed suddenly, barge shipment to the Gulf. The railroad policy had reduced their market options. They thought it would eventually drive them out of business (and in the long run, also cost the railroad business). Based upon what I understood, I supported them in their concerns.

In the hospitality car, the shippers were organized and aggressive in their attack on the railroad's new policy. They felt justified in their outrage; in their view, the railroad was about to put them out of business, which would send their communities into a downward spiral.

I had been away when the new pricing structure policy had been announced. I had heard about it in the local grain elevator and understood its implications for the shippers, but I didn't appreciate how angry the shippers were. Nor had I been aware of their plan to confront the railroad's president that evening.

The shippers came at him from all sides. The president

was caught off-guard without detailed knowledge of the recent pricing change. This wasn't the scenario for the evening he had envisioned; the situation had suddenly become a real problem for him, one that might jeopardize the future of his company. His eyes flashed around the room, landed on me and he saw his chance to recover. In a loud voice he told me, "Get back to Chicago right now and get this problem fixed by tomorrow!"

> **The prevailing attitude was that railroading would be a lot more fun if we didn't have the shippers and their complaints.**

I was dumbfounded. We were in the middle of nowhere and it was nearly midnight. How could I possibly get back to company headquarters in Chicago that night? And even if I did, there was little I could do. Pricing policies weren't set by the railroad's marketing division, where I reported, but by the pricing department, which was run by a demon who listened to no one. I was going to tell *him* what to do?

I wanted to help the shippers, but at the same time I didn't want to pretend I could do something for them I couldn't. I knew that the shippers would be counting on me, and I felt like I was being set up to let them down. I was also aggravated that the president was implying to the shippers, my new friends, that I had had something to do with this problem. I wanted to set the story straight, explain the reality to everyone in order to avoid certain failure, but I wasn't sure how to proceed.

The shippers were all nodding at one another, impressed by their ability to make demands on the president and by his dramatic response to those demands. He seemed to mean business.

Tentatively, I found my voice. "Well, I don't really think it's that simple," I said, looking for a way out. "Jim Hogley, the head of pricing, will have to be told to change his policy—I'm not sure he's going to take that message too well from me. Plus any pricing changes have to go to the Interstate Commerce Commission for approval, so Jim will need to know this change is a priority if it's going to happen in a reasonable amount of time." I was picturing myself back at headquarters, seeing the support I would need, wanting to get that lined up, mostly oblivious to how my comments might come across to the president and shippers.

> The shippers started rolling their eyes, giving each other that look.

The shippers started rolling their eyes, giving each other that here-we-go-again look. Their adulation of the president abruptly halted. Understandably, the president didn't like being challenged by me in front of a room of people he wanted to impress. I suddenly found myself without a friend in the room.

He grabbed his administrative aide and told him in a voice loud enough for everyone on the car to hear, "Get her off this train now and onto a plane to Chicago tonight." To me he snarled, "When I get back to Chicago tomorrow, this had better be settled!"

The aide took my elbow and escorted me off the train. He didn't say much on the way to his car. Finally he said, "I don't think we're going to find a flight to Chicago tonight—I guess I should drop you at your hotel. Why don't you give Paul a call in Chicago and tell him what's going on?" I nodded dumbly.

Paul was the head of marketing and a guru in the company, well-liked and the person everyone seemed to approach for informal advice. He was something of a maverick; most of his shirts were frayed at the collar, he had a giant gold screw on his desk emblazoned with "Screw You," and he ate peanuts all day long, throwing the shells on the floor. Usually when I happened by his office, he was there with several other people, sitting around, relaxed, exchanging ideas. He wasn't my boss, he was my boss's boss, but I agreed instinctively that he was the one to consult in my "emergency." I called him from my hotel.

Paul was surprisingly chipper for being awakened when I reached him and recounted what seemed a horror story of enormous magnitude. He asked me to describe exactly what had happened. After I was through he chuckled.

"Don't worry about it," he said. "Get a good night's sleep and come back to Chicago tomorrow. What happened just means you've joined the club."

"The club?" I asked, bewildered.

"There's a group of us, we've all been thrown out of a room at one time or another by the president. Once I got lifted up by my shirt collar and hauled out of his office. It's no big deal, though you're the first to be thrown off a train. I guess it probably wasn't too much fun, but I suppose he had had a couple, and tomorrow I doubt if he'll remember a thing. We'll sort it all out when you get back."

I wanted to mention that I thought the shippers would remember, but I decided to be grateful for the easy spin he put on the evening's events.

Weeks later I learned that the president had demanded I be fired for insubordination. Paul had refused to go along with this as had his boss, and the matter was eventually dropped. Then the bankruptcy court turned down the company's reorganization plan and more urgent problems than my fate had to be addressed.

The experience led me to decide that authority and aggravation often went together. People in organizations who had power could be easily aggravated for no good reason other than that something wasn't the way they wanted it. Similarly, they made decisions without having all the details they needed, which often made work aggravating for others—more difficult than it needed to be.

All of this, I decided, was teaching me a lot about the business world and how unsafe it could be. I thought it had been promising to be taken under the wings of the Iowa shippers, but it turned out that I was "disposable" in the drama of corporate survival. CEOs could be tyrants—individuals who wielded power and could be mean and ill-informed. It wasn't so safe to speak up—that could make the situation worse. If there happened to be a nice guy around, someone like free-spirited Paul, their protection could ease the way, but I had been lucky. I couldn't always count on a Paul being around. I would have to take care of myself. I would have to be tough. And good. And care-

ful about what I said and to whom. I loved the business
world—the problems to be solved, the strategies, the
opportunities. But it would be a lonely path, as, in the
end, I decided, I had only myself to take care of me.

The railroad was never successful at reorganizing, and
ultimately was disassembled and sold for scrap. It had
been an education, I told myself. I had made some mistakes but not costly ones.

But the transportation industry appealed to me. In
those days, the risk of an industry moving offshore was
high—but domestic freight transportation was an industry that couldn't really be moved offshore. On the other
hand, while the industry held strong appeal, consulting
would expose me to many different companies—so I
headed next for a consulting practice that specialized in
transportation, armed with my tough attitude and a vow
to stay self-reliant.

For a long time, I did the "I walk alone walk," focused
on delivering what I had promised, and learned how to
avoid aggravating agitators while not seeing how my own
style mirrored the style I was avoiding.

At one point a boss attempted to give me feedback.
"Your work is excellent," he said. "However, if you could
be a little friendlier with people, you'd have more friends
and could get more accomplished." I said nothing in
response, but internally my mind was operating at full
speed dismissing him and his ideas. 'Ha! If I wanted
friends, I wouldn't work,' I thought. 'It's easy to keep your
distance with people at work—*that's what I like about
work.* I learned a long time ago to depend on myself. Sure,
people don't like my ideas sometimes. But I always have

> **I have slowly come to realize that the belief that we're separated from others is an illusion.**

my data and my facts and am on solid ground when I take a position. I don't always win the argument, but I always have a good case. Besides, who has time to chat? There's too much work to do.'

I have slowly come to realize that the belief that we're separated from others is an illusion. We think we are separate because we have separate bodies. And that no one can know what we feel inside of our own body. But I've come to appreciate that we all feel pretty much the same way when we are hurting and want to be free of pain—free to create what we see as possible. To be all we can be. And work is one place where we can work this out.

What we do does affect others and in this way we are all deeply connected. We are learning how to come together, leverage one another's assets fully, and collaborate to create what we want to create. In the process we "upset" and "trigger" one another and this serves the larger lesson which we are learning, which then expands what it is possible to create.

Understanding this is nirvana-like to me; it means

that whatever is happening is all right because everything is an opportunity for learning. Corporations are wonderful environments because once we get conscious about this learning opportunity so much creativity is possible within big organizations.

For me, this learning path started when I began to admit the truth—that I was lonely and scared and it hurt to feel this way. When I finally did, I could also admit it was burdensome to walk alone because work projects didn't

always work out. Then I'd get depressed and it was a rough ride to rev my enthusiasm back up. Connecting more deeply with others, being willing to be supported by others has lightened my load considerably.

I was able to surface this truth about myself because others I knew had seen it in themselves before me and expressed it, and I could recognize myself in the experiences they related. This is why, in organizations where there is "trauma and drama"—long-standing feuds between individuals and groups, for example—often all that is required to ease the conflict is to recognize what each person is experiencing. When a group sees how individually they all deeply influence one another's common experience, and they clearly state what alternative experience they want to create together, grace enters the room.

When we realize that what we feel, others feel too, we realize that we are part of something bigger than ourselves; we recognize some process unfolding in which we all search for some meaningful connection, with ourselves, with others, with the purpose of our life. Loneliness and other "negative" experiences can assist us in making the connection with our purpose and taking steps to create the experiences we want.

When we do, all the pain—the fear, the despair, the hurt, the anger—doesn't disappear. These "negative" feelings are part of life.

But our attitude changes. Instead of blaming others for "making us" feel this way, we use our inner experience to discover how it is we are creating the illusion of separation from others—how we are judging ourselves and others "bad" or "wrong." We discover our next "learning." For me, this path has been nirvana-like, even though there are challenging moments when I sometimes forget I am learning. One client, Bob, was especially instructive in this way.

Bob was an executive at a large multi-divisional consumer products firm which had hired our company to assist them in their operations. In an effort to improve the return on their assets, a good deal of pressure had been put on the various company divisions to reduce inventory levels. Inventory is after all an asset, and so reducing inventory, all else being equal, is a way to improve the return on assets, or the earnings per asset dollar.

> **We realize that what we feel, others feel too.**

The pressure to reduce inventory at this company had subsequently led to low stock levels so that its warehouses were sometimes out of product when orders arrived. As a result the company would lose sales. For this reason,

inventory management is an ongoing challenge that all merchandise-supplying businesses face. The company wanted to find the right balance between reducing the investment in inventory and maintaining a sufficiently high level of stock to ensure adequate order fulfillment for its customers.

Bob had delivered right away, assembling a core-team of five bright and experienced managers to direct the project. He had also quickly assembled a second team of thirty-five individuals, at least one from every company division and several from the corporate office. This second group would ultimately be responsible for achieving buy-in for the project's recommendations on inventory management throughout the organization. Getting this structure in place was a remarkable achievement that laid an early foundation for broad participation and success.

A good part of what the company needed to do was conduct a fairly standard analysis, "trading-off" inventory investment and product availability. The company wanted to set goals for product availability and inventory investment reduction, then look at performance over time to see how things were going.

As with a number of companies with whom we had worked, the team knew the company had the necessary data in its computer to perform the needed inventory analysis, but individuals on the team lacked the resources to get at the data easily.

The company was frugal and resources for information technology were tight. At our first project meeting, one of the core-team members stated with exasperation, "I've been asking for inventory levels for my division's top sales items for sixteen weeks. How difficult can it be to get that? How can I make business decisions without being able to get my hands on basic information?"

At many companies for whom we worked, frustration over the lack of good information ran high, a feeling made all the worse because people knew the data was "on the premises." They just couldn't get at it. Our approach when confronting this problem was to take a company's raw data and load it onto our computer. Once we had the data, we could refine the analysis no matter what we learned during the study.

Over the years, my partner had become extremely proficient at retrieving and analyzing data. Once he has the data, and solves the problem at hand, he can then explain to a programmer how to get a company's internal systems to produce the same information on a regular basis. The term for this is "rapid-prototyping" and my partner does this with such speed that it is almost like he and his computer are having a technological dialogue.

To create the analysis the company had in mind, we anticipated the need to fit large amounts of company data on our personal computers. Downloading a year's worth of company orders would be the byte equivalent of loading twenty-five sets of the *Encyclopedia Britannica*. But we have easily handled downloads of this size in the past.

Before embarking on the project, the company had interviewed a number of consulting firms in addition to ours; we had been the only one to convince the company of our capability to do the project. This was partly because we had already done a similar exercise for another firm. So we moved along to the actual work.

So, we are at an early meeting with the team, debating exactly how to approach the mainframe data downloading, and I begin to suspect that Bob is aggravated. I am noticing his clipped speech and his clenched jaw as he considers what is being said by the various participants. My partner and I are anxious to get off to a good start, yet we need to stay on track with a project approach we know will work.

Our company's usual tactics for downloading data from another company's mainframe is to obtain a small data sample, look at it, then make an intelligent request for a larger sample sufficient to meet our analytical needs. This approach is grounded in experience; we have yet to receive a "clean" download from a company, one without mistakes in process or information (made inadvertently by company programmers in data extraction). Thus, we review a small data sample, like a week's worth, which reveals errors more readily. Then, once we detect errors made by the programmers in extracting the data, we can give corrective guidance to them for a larger download.

Before we can fully outline our plan, however, Bob is nixing it. "I don't think you appreciate how tight information technology resources are in this place," he says. "There's no way I can ask the information technology group (IT) for two downloads, a small then larger one. We've got one downloading shot and one only and it's going to take every favor I'm owed to even get that. IT is overloaded; everyone in IT will have to work twelve hours a day over the next six months. The whole reason we have you for this project is the lack of IT resources, so we have to keep their involvement with the project to a minimum."

Everyone in the room nods in agreement. Each person has his own IT horror story to tell. We know that Bob and his political connections offer the only chance for the project. And we know his team will defer to his call in this area. We too have decided to rely on his instincts about the best way to get things done in his organization.

My partner and I consult with one another and decide

that if Bob's way is the only one that offers the chance of success, then we'll have to go with it. My partner is apprehensive about the single download, however, and expresses his fears. If we get only one download and there is a problem with the data, then what happens?

Bob responds quickly. In such a case, he says, he'll have the *right* to go back to IT and ask for additional information.

Clearly, Bob is aggravated because we've questioned his approach. His attitude says, "This is the only way to do it, so just get on board and stop arguing with me." I recognize his driver energy, his sureness about his own point of view, his annoyance with others who don't share it, his irritation with questions that, he believes, can only slow his progress; all of which point to the personality of a results-oriented achiever.

Achievers know how to push toward goals. They know how to lay out a plan for realizing a particular end and how to blow away obstacles in their path. This is why questioning their approach can annoy them — they perceive the questioning as an obstacle. They can be absolutely convinced their approach must be followed or a particular effort will fail. This conviction, this drive, is a powerful strength. It's also a weakness if taken too far because it can assume the form of an unwillingness to consider other people's ideas. And in that case, the result will only be as good as the driver's ideas.

Trying to get a driver to stop and consider approaches different from the one he or she believes in feels like trying to get a freight train moving at full throttle to slow down by putting yourself in its path. I remember vividly the first time I considered the possibility that someone else's approach might work better than a well-thought-out idea of mine. I felt shocked by the admission of the possibility—the severity of my response indicated to me how much I felt I had to run the show—yet ultimately it was wonderful when I was finally able to let go of my need to be in control and share the burden of responsibility with others.

Since I also have a driver personality, I tried to be careful of getting wedded too closely to my ideas when Bob challenged them. I didn't want to get in an ego struggle with him about whose approach is best. I also wanted him to stay calm and see us as flexible and easy to work with. So I let go of needing to further explain our approach to the download and agreed to go along with him. At the time, I wasn't fully able to see what was being set in motion by Bob's aggravation and my wanting to stay safely out of the way of his forcefulness.

Whether going along with someone is a good idea depends more on the intention—why we go along—than it does with going along per se. In this case, my decision to go along with Bob had to do with my intention to try to win him over and my desire to avoid a confrontation early in our relationship. Our company paid a price for this deference, however. If we had been more committed to our shared goal than to Bob's opinion of us, the project might have gone more smoothly than it eventually did. Once a "going along" ground rule had been established, we had to "shout" twice as loudly to be heard at all.

> **Whether going along is a good idea depends on the intention behind it.**

The next step in preparing our download request requires our getting together with IT to have the system explained to us. This will take a whole day, Bob insists. We feel this is excessively long, but once again we defer to his sense of things. Bob also has definite ideas about which IT person we should meet with. It is easy to just go along with his thinking.

We arrive for the meeting—and discover confusion. The IT individual Bob had wanted us to meet has left a message saying that he won't be able to join us. It seems that Bob hadn't inquired sufficiently about his availability. Bob then takes the better part of the morning reorganizing the day's schedule. It is at this point that I become aware of the productivity price we've been paying for being tentative about challenging Bob's need to make all the decisions.

At last we gather with the IT experts who offer us general information about the system—an orientation. But my partner requires exact technical data. Pretty soon I realize that the meeting has little value for him. He has stopped jotting down notes—in fact, he is nodding off. Feeling embarrassed, I ask him, "So, is this discussion helping you?"

"Not really," he answers, stating the obvious.

"So what would help," I ask, hoping to draw him out.

"I'm not sure," he says with a puzzled expression. His precision is a gift, but this is one time I wish he'd make up an answer regardless of whether it was accurate.

"Well, you have a whole room full of people who want to help you learn how their system works," I say, wanting to fill the silence. "Everyone is willing to help. But you need to tell us what you need to know to understand the system." This, thankfully, hits the mark.

My partner shifts into gear and puts three specific requests on the table: one for a description of the data fields, another for a complete copy of the file describing the company's products, the third to have someone sit down with him, go into the system and track an order he had written down a few days earlier when we toured the company warehouse. This had become his "pet order," a shipping request he wanted to trace as it made its way through the company's order-fulfillment process.

The IT people look puzzled. My partner's approach isn't the one they would have followed to understand the system. But they are helpful nonetheless and the day ends productively for us; we leave with a fifteen-inch stack of computer printouts with the file description, a promise of a disk containing a couple of key files, and numerous insights gleaned about his pet order.

When I arrive at my office the next morning, there is a memo waiting for me. My partner has indeed been productive—he has digested the file descriptions and is beginning to understand the system.

My partner has a conscientious work style. Psychologically speaking, this means that he has a core fear of making a mistake. To avoid error, therefore, his approach to his work is methodical: he makes a rough guess about a problem's solution, then, testing various hypotheses and getting better data on key factors, he continually improves on his assessment. He couches every answer in terms of his comfort with the answer. Since he never claims an answer is "perfect", only "about right", he doesn't overly invest in the time to produce perfect answers. He's very good at this approach, and it has been a way for him to manage his fear without engaging in "analysis paralysis".

Bob's warning that the download request had to be stated perfectly—that we had only one chance to get the information we required—naturally made my partner anxious. I noticed he was spending days and days working on getting the request perfect. At the same time, I was keeping an eye on the project budget. We hadn't planned for this much time to specify the download request, but since everything rode on a correct download, it was difficult to pull back.

So, we are now finally ready to submit our download request, which is many pages long. We set up a conference call with IT to go over the request that had been faxed to them previously. They look it over, and we talk briefly about our problem—the difficulty of knowing exactly what data we'll need to download before we've worked with the data, a catch-22 situation. Then they make a startling suggestion: "Why don't we send you all the data we have for a week," they offer. "You can work with it and then you'll know what to ask for." They have, in other words, agreed to do two downloads, thus following our standard procedure! We're delighted, of course. I have a fleeting regret about the days of wasted effort trying to get the download request perfect, but their offer appeals to us because our experience tells us that this approach will work.

Later, Bob is defensive. "This is the only way we could ever have gotten the two downloads," he says, "the idea of it had to come from them. If we had suggested it, they would never have agreed to do it."

Maybe—there is no sure way to know. More importantly, though, I realize that we still haven't gained any ground with Bob; he's still trying to reinforce the idea that he knows best. But we let the matter rest.

The project continues to unfold. When individuals in the company see what we're able to do with the data, which now provides detailed information on inventory and product availability and how the two are related, they're ecstatic. Expectations for what can be achieved are exceeded. Even IT starts to attend newly formed meetings to discuss information problems, and wholeheartedly endorses the project. The number of participating company divisions increases and there's talk about setting a new high-water mark in the industry for the way product availability and inventory levels can be managed.

Closer to home, every step in the project's realization seems to take longer than we anticipate. Bob continues to make microscopic decisions about our approach; he's constantly second-guessing us, which complicates the work we're trying to do. Bob and I have disagreed so many times about process that he begins to make decisions unilaterally, announcing them via email to the team and sending copies of his memos to us. We've become entirely reactive, responding to him decision by decision, not discussing the underlying issue of who will lead the technical aspects of the project for fear of how he'll receive this input.

Bob is convinced that he must make the decisions about how the project gets done, and though he doesn't have the expertise to do so, we say nothing. We also don't convey the impact his position is having on our productivity. He doesn't see how a decision on his part adds hours of work for us and could actually jeopardize the project's success. When he asks us to expand the scope of the project, we do so, but this time we're realistic about the real time and cost of performing the work. Bob doesn't receive this news well—he's convinced we're not being fair in our estimate of the time the work takes.

I am dumbfounded. It's the first time in my experience that a client is so pleased with the quality of the work we're doing yet so aggravated about the project in general. I decide it's way past time for me to step back and look at my role in this drama, to see what I need to learn to resolve the situation.

The first step as I see it is to get clear on what I really feel about Bob's behavior.

This takes some work. There is a lot of emotion churning inside so I have to spend some time with each feeling and the thoughts connected to them, weighing and evaluating, seeking the thing in Bob that really pushes my buttons. In fact, there are so many things I don't like about what Bob does that I keep wanting to make *him* the issue and leave it at that. The Piper Principle (described in Chapter 3) has taught me that the vehemence of my reaction to Bob's behavior indicates a negative judgment I've made about myself that I don't see—and whose revelation will help me to deal with Bob successfully. But it's a challenge to stay on track and discover my blind spot. I know that when I identify the thing about Bob that annoys me the most, I'll have the key to what I'm concealing from myself about myself. Then I'll be a member of the AAA Club—able to appreciate the usefulness of aggravation, his and mine. And I'll be able to approach him effectively about the issues I see.

I keep "trying things on." Is what annoys me most about Bob the fact that he keeps making decisions without consulting us first? That he thinks he knows what needs to be done better than we do? That he sends email announcing decisions that affect us, without consulting us first? All of this behavior seems so disrespectful.

Finally I have it. The thing that really bothers me

about him is that he is so darn negative all of the time, so wrapped up in his own...aggravation. No matter how well everything is going, no matter that the project is being exceedingly well-received, Bob is invariably focused on the one small thing that might go wrong, the disaster that he imagines is just up ahead. I wonder if it's possible for him to experience success, he wants so to focus on the problems, real or imagined.

> **No matter how well everything is going, Bob is invariably focused on the one small thing that might go wrong.**

And right then I hear a voice in me that's exactly like Bob's—the aggravated voice that always dismisses the wins and instead focuses on the losses, imagined or real, focuses on the negative. It's the first time I'm aware of this voice, which I now realize has run my life to a great extent, but which until then I'd never been aware of. It's a shock! I don't think of myself as someone who is frequently aggravated or negative, but the more time I spend in reflection, the more I see how familiar this negative voice is. And I see how the dark energy of being upset with others has created distance between myself and others. It's an odd thing—a strikingly familiar yet entirely surprising discovery.

No wonder Bob grates on me. He's demonstrating an aspect of myself I hadn't seen, hadn't wanted to see, had avoided seeing—an aspect I'd disowned to the point of not knowing it existed.

The thing about aggravation is that it's similar to enthusiasm in terms of the energy it requires. While enthusiasm is energy directed toward a goal, aggravation is a similar force directed away from or against it—against an idea, person, or situation. We have a choice about how to direct our energy, I recognize. We can direct our energy for a goal, or against something or someone. We don't have to be trapped by its negative manifestation.

I'm pleased by this discovery and inside I ease up. Now that I've seen what Bob is showing me about myself, I no longer need to make him the problem. I can stay clear on what is required to make the project successful. I can take responsibility for communicating to Bob what I think is required to make the project work and take responsibility for being heard, even if confrontation is required to do so. I can rely on my experience and articulate what needs to be done from my perspective. I can even let go of whether or not our company's recommendations are followed; my only job is to present information, to clarify options. And—great relief—I can stop trying to prevent Bob from making inappropriate decisions, because in reality, managing his behavior is not my job. I'm able, in other words, to stay clear about my own sense of what is needed for success and keep my attention and communication focused on that.

A couple of days later Bob recommends that the next meeting, which involves the larger team and at which its final results are to be presented, be delayed a month. He cites as the reason for this that our company hasn't received information we requested, and this information is absolutely necessary, he says, for the meeting to be productive. But his understanding of the situation is out of date—we *have* received the data.

In any case, the decision to postpone an important

meeting like the upcoming one is radical and not something we agree with. Delaying the meeting will slow the project's building momentum and the implementation of its recommendations. And, equally important, it will force us to stop working for a month meaning that we'll lose our sharpness regarding the intricacies of the data. As I see it, a delay is not only unnecessary, it will harm the project.

I let Bob know how we feel about postponing the meeting. Bob expresses frustration and says that, in any case, it's not likely that the meeting will be held as planned. He has, I realize, his own reasons for wanting to postpone the meeting, but, in light of my new learning, I don't feel the need to fight or to win—only to do my best to have our thinking heard. I find that I am detached from his reaction, seeing it, but not taking it personally. I realize that my willingness to handle my inner issue is keeping me in balance and keeping me productive even as Bob is going out of balance.

I jokingly let Bob know that as difficult as it is to encounter his wrath, I'll keep letting him know when his decisions adversely affect the project, as I see it, because a successful result efficiently achieved is the goal. My attitude stays "for the goal" rather than "against Bob." And it works; I'm no longer trying to bulldoze him; I just keep coming back to the real goal—the project's success—so he's not threatened by my comments. He begins to consider what I am saying. And he decides to keep the meeting date after all. He communicates this to the team, stating that he and we have managed to work through the difficulties.

We're ready to present a draft of the final results at the

meeting; it will include the specific recommendations we have for each of the company's divisions. Therefore, we will need the core team's input and review first. Core team members have been busy traveling the past few weeks, so the meeting will be their first chance to review the details as we present them. While there are no surprises, the team has an appetite for details; their willingness to dig into them in the past has enabled them to stand solidly behind the work that is being done. Therefore, we let Bob know it will be helpful to get the team's input on the report page by page and that this should take about four hours to do.

The night before the core team meeting, a note slides under the door of my hotel room. It's from Bob and contains an agenda for the next day. There are seventeen items on the list, most of which don't relate to our project. I hope, therefore, that there'll be enough time to cover all the project items.

I leave a message on Bob's answering machine, reminding him of the time we will need for our review. I feel myself becoming aggravated; Bob's been on an emergency job for two weeks and hasn't been available to talk about the project. Yet here he goes again, in this case publishing an agenda without talking to us first and getting up-to-date on where things are with the project.

Clearly I haven't gotten to the bottom of the well on my aggravation. But I feel that I'm getting close; I just need to step back and do some thinking—and feeling.

I take a breath and explore the emotion I'm having at the moment. What is it? I let the feeling intensify and suddenly an awareness comes forward. I realize that the aggravation I'm experiencing actually feels like a protective shield, a barrier against feeling vulnerable. And as I recognize this, I feel the shield drop away and experience that sense of emotional nakedness. It seems related to feeling unappreciated, insufficiently valued. Since I always want to avoid these painful feelings—this vulnerability—I see I do so by trying to ensure that nothing I do, or anyone else does, is wrong. I'm sad as I realize this, at how my need to protect myself against feeling vulnerable creates distance from myself and others. I feel sad that I've always needed this protection.

Once again, I realize that I've given Bob a hard time rather than acknowledge certain feelings in myself. I've been constantly on the attack with him, looking for the fallacy of his approach. I've been quick to see what he's doing wrong—which, I realize, is often the thing I've done with myself. In fact I had been doing it just now—making myself wrong for wanting to protect myself from certain feelings that were uncomfortable to feel.

Now my negative emotion lifts and a sense of balance is restored. I feel lighter—I feel joy in going to this new level of self-awareness. I take another look at the agenda. I can see that actually it's not bad. I can appreciate Bob's skill in listing all the items that the team might want to discuss. As I look again, I see that we are listed early on the agenda. I see that some of the items involve topics I don't know about and they may well be topics that require the group's input. I also appreciate that we are ready for the meeting and the group will be fascinated by what we have to say. I spend a few moments imagining the ideal day with the core team. I see that the agenda is fine; it will work.

And it does. We have the time we need. Bob is excited by the information we present, saying over and over how important it is that we take the time necessary even if it means not getting to other items on the agenda. The comments the team members make are supportive and helpful. I realize I'm experiencing my ideal scene. I leave the meeting feeling quite peaceful about where things are on the project and with my relationship with Bob, which seems more authentic than it's ever been. I acknowledge my willingness to look within, explore my feelings, rather than "correct" Bob, which, I see now, would not have been at all productive.

All this has come about because I was able to see how I can use the experience of feeling aggravated to reveal a personal blind spot, rather than making the person "causing" that emotion bad.

I use aggravation in exactly the same way these days, to indicate the existence of a blind spot. When I'm at peace, I trust everything will work out fine. I don't need to be in control of, or agree with, what is going on in a given situation. I can watch what's going on objectively and offer my perspective. I'm clear about my contribution, whatever it may be, and I know there's a story unfolding that is bigger than I am, one whose meaning will be revealed in good time, a story that connects us all.

When, however, I'm not in a place of peace and self-trust, or if I find that I've been or am continually making someone wrong, or judging another negatively, or collecting evidence, I know that it is time to pay my membership dues to the AAA club. At such times I can mistakenly act as if I should be in control—and I see that this assumption comes from fear of failure or fear that I won't receive the approval I seek. It is motivational to understand the issue in these terms because, rather than making myself or others wrong, and separating from them in the process, it makes the situation instead about learning how to be more effective. And that is something I feel highly motivated to do.

Aggravation, I now see, is my internal alert; recognizing it means I can get back on the path of inner peace by paying my dues—surfacing and acknowledging to myself what feelings are present.

Sometimes, even with this insight, I notice that I am still resistant to a full exploration of what is going on; I see myself postponing it, preferring the familiar comfort of holding on to my feeling of aggravation about someone or something else. During those times, I am learning to encourage myself forward by accepting that I am learning, rather than feeling aggravated with myself. This level of acceptance with regard to my own process brings me to a new level of honesty with myself. And I know that this process is bringing me to new levels of honesty and intimacy in my relationships with others. And this recognition brings another measure of peace.

‡ ‡ ‡

We have recently started a new project with a new client involving their processes of developing and launching new product ideas. It is early on, but already we have been warned about "the man at the top." Fear of this individual runs rampant through the company. He is clearly an aggravating agitator of a most intimidating type. My trepidation is familiar, but I know that he is on my path for a purpose that will be revealed. Already I am learning. I am clear that the anxiety I feel about him is based on fear, the fear is that I won't do what I should and will get hurt. Just seeing this eases the situation remarkably. I don't have to do "it" right. I will do my best, and whatever happens will be what happens. I will handle whatever comes up as it comes up and I will use what happens for learning. If I fantasize about the future, it will be about "ideal scenes" I hold.

I also discover that there is much to appreciate in what our company is doing in this new situation. We are speaking openly with the individuals we are working with about the productivity consequences of "over-management." We are exploring their feelings about it, and we are engaged in a highly productive way in supporting them through their challenges. The work is intimate and rewarding. We have much of value to offer. I am staying conscious of being *for* the goal rather than *against* anyone or anything, staying

connected with myself, staying in relationship with others.

I know I'm heading down a new track of learning. I don't know what this trip will be like—but I do know that there will be wins and learning opportunities along the way. I remind myself that I am here to be of service and to learn; the AAA Club express is leaving the station, and I am grateful to be on the train—to have the opportunity to use my skills and to learn. I see that I am embracing the journey with gratitude in my heart and with a willing spirit. With delighted enthusiasm at seeing this, I head for my seat.

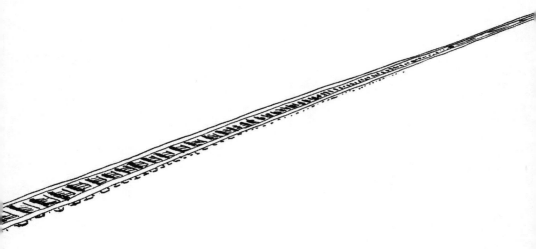

CHAPTER 6

A **Hole** IN THE **Road**

Learning the
Lesson
so the Test
Disappears

▼

Whatever
satisfies the
soul is truth.

—

WALT WHITMAN

A **Hole** IN THE **Road**

KNOWING I shouldn't do something, yet doing it anyhow, is like stepping in a hole on a familiar path. Darn! I knew that hole was there, yet I stepped in it again! In the past, I'd be hard on myself because "I should've known better." I'd tell myself, "Jeez, how many times are you going to fall into that same darn hole?"

For example, when I'd complain to a customer service person, and sharpen my tone to let them have it—so they'd realize I was really offended by some screw-up that had cost me time and trouble—I was falling into a hole, repeating behavior that didn't work. I was responding before I'd consciously considered whether doing so was a good idea. My reaction was automatic, a response to a perceived injustice—and it took me smack into unproductive behavior. Later, when I was calm, I'd remind myself that the problem, whatever it was, wasn't the service person's fault, that they were there to help, and that being rude wasn't the best way to engage their support. I knew all this, so why did I behave otherwise?

Repetitive "don't-work" patterns like the one I've described—upset feelings coupled with unproductive behavior—are an indication that a learning opportunity is present.

Conscious awareness of an unproductive pattern is the first step toward that learning and an elevation in productivity. Resolution comes when I identify the self-judgment that underlies such patterns, forgive it, and then let it go.

In the situation above, this would mean untangling my inner experience—thoughts and feelings—in relation to what had gone on outwardly:

Realizing the difference between what happened on the "factual" level...

> *It's the 3rd time in a row that the bill has reflected the same wrong amount.*

And what happened on the mental level, the thoughts about it...

> *This should have been taken care of by now. Is no one listening to me?*

And feeling the underlying emotion that the thought produces...

> *Irritation and anger at being ignored.*

And seeing the underlying irrational belief/ judgment...

> *If I were really important, you would take care of me.*

And the core fear underneath that...

> *I'm not important—not significant—not worth paying attention to or being taken care of.*

Realizing that I am the one holding this judgment against myself, and I can let it go…

I forgive myself for judging myself as not significant, not worthy of being paid attention to. The truth is that my worth is not determined by how others respond to me. I am learning to attend to myself and communicate what I need in ways that are respectful—to myself and others.

The personal evidence that learning like this has happened—that misinterpretations and negative self-judgments are being corrected—is that when a "triggering" event occurs, I respond differently than I would have in the past—I respond without the emotional upset. I stay productive and effective.

However, even more is possible. When healing takes place at a deep level, the triggering events that are our "holes in the road," our tests, no longer occur. These tests have served their purpose and are no longer needed in "Earth school." The productivity implications of this are staggering. However, it takes sophisticated inner reflection and communication skills to realize this benefit and a high commitment to learning how to reach goals with greater grace and ease. To fully commit to this path—the path to corporate nirvana—we must be willing to reflect neutrally on whether our behaviors work or don't work, and, in the latter case, experiment with new behaviors to see if they work better. Often this experimentation feels risky.

Sometimes in the past when I made a "mistake"— when I did something and perceived the consequences of

that as bad—I felt that I was being punished. My interpretation was that the consequence represented punish-
ment for my mistake. This can lead to wanting to avoid
mistakes and expecting others to behave similarly. From
this perspective, the risk of stepping outside one's comfort
zone to learn seems, well, risky.

Certainly this is reinforced in a right-wrong workplace
environment where fear of retribution is used by managers
to attempt to control employees (which, finally, can't be
done) and eliminate unproductive behaviors. In these
organizations, risk-taking, innovation, and honest information are often in short supply. What is in ample supply
is blaming, complaining, evidence-gathering and playing
it safe.

On the other hand, a learning mode starts with a
belief that what happens is about learning. This model
doesn't deny the consequences of behavior, just its con-
demnation. In a learning environment, we still need to
evaluate what works and what doesn't—but this occurs
from a learning orientation. This perspective encourages
openness, honesty and learning how to reach goals ever
more productively.

For me, adopting a learning orientation has been especially challenging in repetitive-learning situations. I might
be aware intellectually that a
repetitive pattern doesn't work,
but it can be challenging to
consider how the pattern
nonetheless serves me.
I know intellectually
that there must be some-

thing on an emotional or unconscious level valuable to learn from the pattern, or I wouldn't be repeating it. But this can be hard to accept. I have found that I must be willing to see how a pattern serves me (for example, allows me to get attention, sympathy, a sense of being in charge, or to feel more important than others) and to use that insight for revealing negative self-judgments. When I see a hole in the road, and I trip and fall in it again and again, I have learned not to make the hole bad, but simply notice instead that falling into it repeatedly is making going down the road with speed difficult.

> **When I see a hole in the road, and I trip and fall in it again and again, I have learned not to make the hole bad.**

I have also learned that unproductive patterns—my holes in the road—relate to core fears about not being worthy enough, safe enough, or talented enough to be cared for in the way I truly wish. The more fearful I've been that my worst fears are true, the more I've run for cover from them in the form of blind spots designed to conceal those vulnerabilities. This running-for-cover is subtly revealed by my falling in the same holes—tripping over my own feet—enacting the same patterns again and again.

I have used this insight with my clients as well. In my consulting assignments I'm often quite aware of how a project or task is perfectly suited to bring about resolu-tion to a bottom-line fear that has tripped an individual time and time again. When our eyes and consciousness are open, we can take advantage of this.

Such an opportunity occurred some years ago when I was facilitating discussions between several senior vice presidents who had been asked to look at their company's marketing and sales organizational structure. Specifically, they were debating which activities should be performed in company headquarters and which could be accomplished in various regional offices around the country.

I was nervous about initiating the project. Carl, one of the vice presidents involved, and I had locked horns a couple of times over the best way to approach certain business discussions. Working with him had been a struggle for me; I felt that he continually tried to take over discussions and run the show. When he was in the room, I found that events didn't flow smoothly. I half suspected he didn't think much of my facilitation capabilities, and I was dismissive of his contribution, feeling he was too theoretical. I also found him unwilling to incorporate or validate perspectives gained by others who had spent more time in the trenches than he had. In other words, I didn't find him open to what I had learned and this had rattled my self-confidence from time to time.

This dilemma felt familiar to me as dilemmas often do to people experiencing them. Talking with Carl reminded me of my first few months in Boston, when I was still green career-wise. At the time the inevitable first question asked me in business situations seemed to be, "What does your father do?" Clearly, networking in Boston in those days meant the opportunity to plug into powerful families. I didn't meet too many people who appreciated that I'd grown up on a small Oregon farm. They'd quickly shift focus to someone with a more promising lineage. Dealing with Carl took me back to those insecure times. In Boston I felt excluded by the natural camaraderie of people who belonged, seemingly, to an exclusive Ivy League club. I envied their self-confidence as I envied Carl's. Around Carl, I felt the need to fake a higher level of confidence than I felt and this "blustering" had not always been productive.

I knew that Carl had his preferred choice of facilitators, people from his Ivy League school, and that my being in the room for a meeting meant he had lost his bid to influence the choice of facilitators. I'd be on edge when he was present because I imagined he was looking for ways to trip me up, to build a case against me. If I had been conscious of the Piper Principle at the time—the idea that we ascribe to others behavior that could be true of ourselves but which we haven't acknowledged as such—I would have had a handle on the fact that "case-building" was something I was also capable of—and, moreover, behavior I'd judged myself harshly for engaging in. My evaluation of Carl's behavior wasn't the problem; making him wrong for it, however, indicated a blind spot in me, one I didn't recognize until sometime later.

Though I saw none of this clearly at the time, I had gotten far enough in my awareness to want to take responsibility for having a productive relationship with Carl. So I called him in advance of the project-launching and asked him whether there was an adjustment I might make in my style that would make it easier for us to work together. He told me that sometimes in meetings he thought that I had my own agenda, one that was different from that of the meeting organizers, and that I needed to stay focused on what they wanted to accomplish. In response, I thanked him for being open and acknowledged the importance of staying on track with what the meeting organizers wanted to accomplish.

Clearly, what Carl was criticizing in me was a window through which I could view his own behavior. Often, in meetings where Carl participated, I did have the impression that what I had been asked to do was out of sync with where he wanted the meeting to go, that *he* had *his* own agenda. Nonetheless, what he said was valuable feedback (as feedback from those whom we irritate can be). His feedback helped me see that there was a more effective and direct way of handling my interactions with him in meetings. When it seemed like his comments were taking us off track, I could pause and revalidate my understanding of the meeting objectives, rather than follow the approach I had generally taken, which was to try to strong-arm Carl into staying in sync with what I understood to be the topic of discussion.

I'm fairly certain this conversation made a difference because Carl seemed to walk into the meeting with a softer step. I know I did, and have continued to use the check-in-first approach whenever I sense I'll be working with someone who would prefer not to be working with me. I inevitably get great feedback from the person in question—they open up, tell me what they feel, and things go smoother. In other words, I go for feedback sooner rather than later, which helps me and others stay productive.

I had been curious about how the vice presidents would approach the challenge to improve the organization's effectiveness by addressing issues of structure, roles, responsibilities, and performance tracking. This was more than idle interest. The keys that would make the company work more effectively would, in my experience, be revealed by the VPs' approach to the restructuring, by what would make this group work more effectively on this challenge. Corporate culture is like that. No matter what door you walk through in an organization, the company culture is readily revealed. And this insight—knowing that corporate culture represents itself everywhere in employee attitudes—had enabled me to quickly see things that had broader applicability in terms of accelerating productivity in organizations.

So while I was facilitating discussions in the company, asking questions, clarifying points, flushing out ideas, and organizing thoughts on flip charts, I was also watching and listening to determine when the group was and wasn't effective and what happened that flipped the switch from one to the other.

Greater group effectiveness can be a matter of something seemingly simple, like members increasing their listening skills or keeping their agreements better. Given information about how it can be more effective, an "undefended" group can then readily adjust its behavior, elevating productivity. But when a group can't grasp this information or can't adjust, it's because it's caught in an unproductive pattern, or group "blind spot." As with individuals trying to understand their unproductive patterns, a group must search for the shared beliefs or fears that hold the pattern in place.

A belief structure is the sum of the beliefs we hold—
what we tell ourselves about the way the world works.
These beliefs are often unconscious—and
we see them as absolute truths, determined
by things beyond our control, rather than
choices we make. Shared belief structures
are commonly called an organization's culture. "It will never change around here!"
"No one is interested in new ideas in this
place." "It's hopeless, why bother?" are
examples of limiting beliefs that can characterize a company's culture. They become self-fulfilling
prophecies because we search for evidence or "proof" that
they are true and we filter the information that is available
so that we give validity to what we believe to be the case.
This mental process reflects the way our brains handle the
huge amount of information available to it moment by
moment—we filter out "unnecessary" information.

> **What would happen if people thought of beliefs as neither right nor wrong?**

I'm often awed by the power of substituting an expan-
sive goal-supporting belief for a limiting one. Just say, "It
will never change around here" with conviction, and then
say with equal conviction, "One person can make a difference" to experience the dramatic effect such a switch has
on enthusiasm and willingness. This is why conscious
management of belief structures can result in huge
increases in productivity. They affect the decisions we
make and our level of enthusiasm for what we do.

Notwithstanding the vast potential of corporate belief-
change, the idea that it's possible to just up and change
one's beliefs, that limiting beliefs can, like worn-out shoes,
be tossed aside with no more thought than they're out of

date, goes beyond what most managers are willing to consider. They have amassed too much evidence to demonstrate that their beliefs are "right."

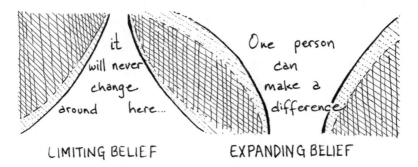

LIMITING BELIEF   EXPANDING BELIEF

What would happen if people thought of beliefs as
neither right nor wrong but rather as supportive or limiting in the context of the goals they set? Such a position
would require us to take more responsibility for the situations we find ourselves in. It would require us to consider
consciously beliefs we hold in relation to our goals—to
examine whether these support us in achieving our goals
or hold us back from doing so. In the latter case, we would
then need to update our beliefs, not only individually, but
in organizations where we participate.

Ferreting out corporate beliefs can be challenging
because the way they operate is so subtle. For example,
many managers and executives have said to me, "What we
need to do in this place is recruit more *drivers,* more
results-oriented, achievement-oriented people. That will
make us successful." This is a belief. And it is not so much
a matter of whether the belief is right or wrong, but
whether it works, in the context of reaching our goals, to
hold it.

In my experience, a belief like this, that others *should* be drivers, can be limiting because it discounts the contribution that other personality styles bring; not surprisingly, it is typical of a driver to presume that "my way is best."

The straightforward DiSC Personal Profile System describes four diverse personality types. It indicates that the core fear of driven individuals is being out of control because that means they may not achieve the results they seek. This resonates with my own experience as a driver. However, being willing to be out of control is often what is required to examine belief structures consciously. The experience of relinquishing a long-held belief can feel initially like free-falling. But letting go in a dramatic way has been necessary for me to learn more effective ways of getting where I want to go.

In the insightful Enneagram system of nine personality types (as put forth by The Enneagram Institute) the achiever, Type 3, can be fearful of whether he or she is valued, and can become caught up with accomplishment as a false path to self-esteem. This type can erroneously believe that individual value must be proven. When they are motivated by a fear like this, they may use strategies of "taking others down a peg," treating them with arrogance or contempt, to "lift themselves up." When they let go of the belief that their value depends on the positive regard of others, they are free to discover where they, and others, can contribute the most. They become self-accepting, genuine, kind, and effective role models.

Being conscious of the beliefs I hold, considering them in the context of whether they support me in the direction I am going or hold me back—and in the latter case, updating my limiting beliefs—has been a powerful tool I use daily. I have also found that a limiting belief is always at the root of a hole-in-the-road experience. When I find myself repeating behavior that prevents me from getting where I want to go easily, I search to identify the limiting belief that the "hole" reflects; it has sometimes taken me several "steps into the hole" to find the limiting belief.

All this came to mind when I was with the vice presidents discussing what organizational changes might help the company be more effective. So I observed their effectiveness. I became particularly attuned to their responses to suggestions about their own effectiveness. But whenever I invited them to look at themselves in this regard, they couldn't; doing so was beyond their frame of reference. They didn't believe they had anything to do with limiting the company's productivity—this blind spot was their hole in the road. So I silently let go of my attachment to getting them to see themselves in this way, reminding myself that I had suspected the group wouldn't be willing to work at a deeper level. What I didn't see at the time, was that this belief reflected my own limiting belief structure—my own hole-in-the-road pattern of feeling "superior" in light of how "un-advanced" others could be and condemning them for it.

One of the issues the group discussed was how to create an empowering environment. "No one here wants to make a decision," said a VP. "I'm not sure we have the talent we need, and the skill levels below us may not be what is required for this organization to be competitive. We have to make sure people know their responsibilities, give them measures for their performance and targets to aim for, and then hold them accountable for doing what they're supposed to. That's empowerment."

I realized the group wanted to tell others how to be more effective without exploring how they might be more effective themselves.

So, they're on a roll, brainstorming about what needs to be done to improve company empowerment. I choose not to mention that in their organization most people are lucky to have two hours a month with their boss to consult about their performance, and that not much coaching or passing on of skills can take place in that time. But I do ask the group how management might be responsible for creating an environment in which there is little feeling of empowerment.

This question annoys Carl. "I'm really tired of hearing that we're the problem," he says. "It's all I hear from people down in the organization"—rank-and-file employees—"that the problem is management's. That just tells me we don't have people who are willing to step forward and make decisions. It's always easier to blame top management for everything. Not being willing to take responsibility is the issue, and I'm really fed up with people complaining about others when they're not willing to act."

Nonetheless, I think my question is valid, and I want to ask Carl more questions concerning his reaction to my question. I hesitate, wondering if I know how to do that effectively. Then I tell myself that to do so would maybe be my agenda, not the group's, so in light of my earlier conversation with Carl, I set my interests aside.

The discussion unfolds and the VPs begin to focus on

the question of organizational structure, especially on what functions should be kept in marketing, which is centralized at the company's headquarters. Should certain activities be divided and moved to decentralized regional offices? A key issue emerges: the poor relationship between the marketing group (which designs product promotional strategies and materials) and the sales force.

The marketing group believes that the sales representatives need to take the time to learn about the promotional programs they have painstakingly designed if the company is to remain competitive and make sales grow. The sales organization feels that many of marketing's programs do not meet their local needs and won't work—that what is needed is greater freedom and a larger budget for sales to develop specific promotional programs tailored to their local audience.

Everyone at the meeting is aware that this marketing/sales debate has gone on in the company for years. The group believes that the issue is one of different points of view—that the truth of the matter depends on where a person sits. They don't see the underlying problem—why the company remains stuck on this particular issue. Their belief is that the problem is endemic, that sales and marketing will always be at odds with one another.

The company has attempted to accelerate sales for years, trying different approaches that result in minor improvements, but it has never addressed the underlying problem so that marketing and sales can communicate effectively, support and value one another, and truly collaborate toward shared goals.

Stuck in its separate camp, sales continues to complain

that marketing is in an ivory tower, spending lots of money designing programs that are never used. Sales continues to build a case for "discretionary money" that can be used to meet local needs.

Marketing, on the other hand, wishes sales could appreciate the breadth of its knowledge—it has data to suggest trends, and programs that have required a good deal of thought to design. If these could just get implemented, then sales would see the value marketing can bring to the table. Marketing shudders at the idea of money being spent haphazardly on a local basis with no way to measure its effectiveness or to ensure that spending meets ethical and legal company standards. For its part, sales is deeply offended by the veiled suggestion that the programs they develop mightn't be ethical or well thought out.

As I hear the familiar positions stated and restated, I think to myself, how many times are they going to try to address the issue by debating structure when the real issue has to do with listening and allowing different perspectives to be valued?

What I didn't see at the time, however, was my own blind spot: my wish to have my own opinions validated by others. I didn't realize that I was taking the group to task for not recognizing its own underlying issues while I was doing that very thing myself.

The group sets the sales versus marketing challenge aside, agreeing that no matter what they do, the issue is not resolvable; they then focus on how to get the level below them clear on performance expectations and responsibilities. The vice presidents want to have statistics in place so it will be clear who is not doing their job properly, and what they need to do to correct their performance—clearly a "fear-based" strategy. They magnanimously agree that long-term measurements of their own performances are appropriate, but what those measurements should be are not clear to them just now.

> **What I didn't see at the time, was that this belief reflected my own limiting belief structure.**

I suggest broadening the number of participants gathered to discuss these issues so that perspectives other than theirs can be put on the table. I offer that the management level just below theirs might provide great input on how their productivity is linked to the way the vice presidents approach their jobs.

"Well, I agree in theory," one vice president says, "but the reality is that certain people will just see what we're doing as political. If you give them any information about what is going on with reorganization, they're going to take it behind the scenes and use it to sabotage the plan before it even gets developed and presented. Collaboration is a nice idea in theory, but it doesn't work in this particular reality."

Carl says to me, "I get what you're saying, about how the issue we're really working with is openness and trust and empowerment and we're not really demonstrating that right now. At some point in the project we may have to address how we can bring more trust forward in the organization—I can see how that would be valuable. But we won't be able to reorganize if we work that way now. What we have to focus on now is structure, process, roles, responsibility, and performance measures. Where we're going with this is important, and we have to be smart or we won't get there. Sometimes you have to use a means that is less than fully desirable to get you to an end that is important and crucial, and I think that this is one of those times."

I realize that Carl is telling me in so many words that I'm following my own agenda, not his, and that it's time to move on.

I had no doubt that the group could relate many stories that proved that Carl's beliefs about trust, cooperation, and sabotage were "true." They had been collecting evidence for years, and were not interested in hearing and considering a perspective that ran contrary to what they "knew" to be true.

Being able to hear fully and appreciate a point of view different from one's own represents a valuable skill. To do this, it's necessary first to be able to let go of the right-wrong model. In this model there are "right" answers, which can be deduced from data or reasoning. If others don't reach the same conclusions we do, then we assume they're dumb, inexperienced, or being political. Following the dictates of this model, it's not possible to acknowledge the value of different views—that different perspectives are exactly what's needed to determine what is actually going on in a given situation. Our views are ours because of all the experiences we have had up to a particular point, the data we have, the assumptions we make. Other people have different experiences and will therefore see things differently from us, a potentially productive distinction. Different views invite us to be creative and synergistic in order to bridge these differences.

The vice presidents couldn't trust others to help build an empowered organization because they felt collaboration would undermine the result they were aiming to achieve. This thinking meant that the new organization would be built from a perspective of fear and distrust, and would take on that personality. Their distrust was deeply embedded in their thinking—to them empowerment was about monitoring people so they wouldn't screw up rather than trusting that individuals are motivated to do a good job naturally.

I suggest these thoughts in the meeting. We go back and forth on the points a couple of times, but they're not buying it.

I withdraw from the exchange, telling myself that I knew this group wasn't there yet, isn't ready to look at their behavior and belief structures in a conscious way. And as I talk to myself about what they could be doing differently, immediately I'm aware of an internal monologue: These guys were limited in this way before I walked in the room, too bad they're not willing to listen...

And then I have an amazing experience. I realize that *I'm* doing it—not listening—myself.

Inside myself, I back down a bit. After all, what I'm proposing—that they invite other company members to join the discussion table—is only one approach. Other approaches might also work. What if the issue really is about the need to make structural organizational changes in relation to marketing and sales? What if the vice presidents are actually on the verge of a solution that would make a difference?

And suddenly I'm quite willing to listen to what the group has to say. So I ask, "I'm wondering if you feel heard right now? I think that maybe I'm not really listening to your point of view."

Right then, right there, I feel my relationship with everyone in the room shift—but most of all with Carl. My honesty has changed the energy in the room, elevated it, and I soon realize that everyone has started to listen, to concentrate on what is being said.

Carl then outlines the new company structure he has in mind. Listening to him, I can appreciate the creativity and innovation of his thinking. I began to hear his views in a different way, wanting to understand what he has to offer. And that meeting (and the meetings that followed) became more synergistic, more collaborative, and more productive.

I had stepped around my hole in the road. I didn't relinquish my perspective—that if this group could challenge itself to change the way it operated it would gain important insights that would enable it to initiate change—but rather than being confrontational and self-righteous, I invited them from time-to-time to consider this view.

> **And then I have an amazing experience. I realize that *I'm* doing it—not listening—myself.**

Toward the end of the meeting, as the group was readying its presentation to peers and top management, Carl opened up. "I think we have a good plan here," he said, "but I just keep coming back to the fear that we won't get a chance to present it, that we won't be heard. That we won't have a chance of getting everyone's buy-in. It's so disillusioning because I know we have a good plan." What Carl said reflected his long experience at the company, but it also shocked me: wasn't he actually revealing his own limiting belief that he wouldn't be heard? There's always real-world evidence to support our limiting beliefs, but which comes first—the evidence or the belief?

To some extent I agreed that there was little chance of buy-in, as buy-in often correlates with participation and the vice presidents had not solicited the participation of top management or others in their thinking. But since Carl had seemed so open in expressing his concern I asked him, in front of the group, "What will you then conclude about yourself if that happens?"

I suppose it was bold of me to ask this question, but when I had started to listen to Carl, I realized I had become "safer" to him—and the safer I became, the more he seemed able to express his vulnerability.

Carl looked at me, paused a heartbeat, and said, "That I don't have what it takes to be a good leader."

I wish I had said many things just then—that he was demonstrating leadership by being open. I wish I had been able to simply acknowledge his concern. I wish I had been able to talk to him about belief systems and the way inner fears are reflected in outer reality. To tell him about the possibility of shifting outer reality by updating the beliefs we hold. But at the time, I didn't think I understood the process well enough to express its operation effectively and I let the moment pass. I was still operating on a belief structure that it wasn't "safe" to let my "lack of expertise" show.

Carl let the moment pass, too. "Well," he said, "we'll do the best we can, in any case."

Weeks passed before I was able to connect with one of the vice presidents to determine how their presentation had gone.

"We only got to page three in it," he said, "then the discussion broke down over the issue of what our original assignment had been. Can you believe it? Every person there, all the top management, had been in the room when they gave us the task. And now suddenly they have amnesia, don't remember why they asked us to do it. We didn't even get a chance to explain our ideas. The whole thing was tabled."

"Wow, that would piss me off," I said. "If I had been asked to take on a project and spent weeks on it while I was already busy anyway, and then I didn't even get a chance to present my conclusion, I would be frustrated—and not very willing to take on the next assignment!"

"Exactly," he said. "I had tons of other work going on that I postponed to do this and all our effort was wasted."

"Are you giving anyone that feedback?" I asked.

He shrugged. "It's this place; people ask you to do something, you do it, and it turns out no one really wanted it done. And then they wonder why there's no empowerment here."

"There needs to be feedback," I said. "Feedback is the first step. Nothing will change unless people speak up and say 'This is not okay with me, this doesn't work.'"

"It won't make a difference," he said. "Nothing will change."

At that moment I saw the whole pattern of what had happened. How the very problem of empowerment the company had wanted to address was mirrored in the way this assignment had gone. I recognized the connection between limiting beliefs—what Carl had feared would happen—and what had "come about"; how a limiting belief can "create" reality, in this case, because the vice presidents were unwilling to include others in their thinking. And I recognized that you can work backwards to use whatever shows up in a situation to discover the keys to achieving success.

I also recognized that I had judged myself harshly for not being able to be more present and effective for Carl and his peers when their limiting beliefs had surfaced. And

I had made myself wrong for not handling the situation more effectively. I could also see that these judgments stood in the way of developing my consciousness. And that it was irrational to feel that I should have been able to handle the vice president more effectively. In fact, I had done the best I could in the moment—if I could have done it differently, I would have. And right then I let the "should have" judgment go. I decided to surrender fully to learning—to let go of expectations that I facilitate better. Instead, I would show up, do my best and trust that whatever happened was for learning. It was a huge shift in perspective for me.

> **I decided to show up, do my best and trust that whatever happened was for learning.**

I also decided to start examining a belief I had long held that I would never be able to explain this "mirror" phenomenon, the Piper Principle, and generally, the way belief structures operated, to my clients in a clear, useful way—one that would catapult them into dramatically different realities based on empowerment rather than limiting beliefs. To show them that they could replace the belief that "I don't have what it takes" with the non-limiting "I'm learning how to do it," and how the projects they undertake help reveal those beliefs, almost as if there were a fated relationship between the two.

I started applying the "belief structure" model more and more to my thinking. I found that when a group or an individual was pursuing a goal, a barrier could arise that would reflect a limiting belief. When the limiting belief was addressed, the goal became easier to achieve and productivity accelerated. I had discovered that there was a relationship between individual beliefs and the success of a project—and individual success more generally. This discovery was challenging because *my* limiting belief—my hole-in-the-road conviction of my own "incapacity" to articulate this model—continued to rear up, requiring attention. But the level of enthusiasm and passion that I felt when exploring the belief-structure model was profound and pushed me forward. I saw how an understanding of the relationship of beliefs to outcomes could make a huge difference in business effectiveness, and I decided to rid myself of my limiting belief rather than capitulate to it. Going forward, I decided to believe that I was learning how to explain these ideas gracefully and easily—and was doing just fine in this learning process.

‡ ‡ ‡

Months later I was able to watch my learning in action. A group of people wanted to spend some time exploring creative problem-solving and out-of-the-box thinking. I had some ideas about how to proceed with this, but wasn't sure I could communicate them effectively. Just as I heard my inner self start to say, "I'm not sure I have what it takes to lead this discussion..." I shifted belief gears to "I have a good idea how to go about this, and the process will give me a chance to learn even more."

At our first meeting, I took the group through various exercises designed to get them past conscious mind and into deeper levels of creative self-expression. I had come to believe that difficult problems can be solved in a blink if we can find a completely new way of considering them. The exercises I had the group do were designed to get them "loosened up", and they soon became comfortable working in different ways. An element of play came into the room and individuals started to see value in relaxing and experimenting with new approaches. I was relaxing too.

After the warm up exercises, I invited the group to identify a difficult problem so that we could try the approach on a real challenge. The group had been struggling for months to define the company's fundamental message to customers. "If," one person in the group stated, "we had fewer than ten words to express our message, and we wanted it to apply to all our customers, across all products and in all situations, what would the message be?"

Every person in the room except me believed that a lot of analysis and hard work would be needed to solve the problem. This belief frustrated the group endlessly as no one had the time to tackle the problem in the systematic fashion they thought was required—and so the problem of creating a single customer message was always pushed aside.

Yet every time group members interacted with customers, promotion managers, sales representatives, or senior management, the unresolved issue of identity seemed to surface—it was at the core of any debate. The company didn't need an advertising slogan—they had that—but an underlying message that would sum up the kind of relationship the company wanted to have with its customers, one that would also unify the organization.

Not having this overarching theme, individuals would argue about which specific marketing strategies and tactics were appropriate, each of which implied a certain fundamental approach to customers. Sales representatives had been making up their own key messages for years (such as "We want to add value!"; "We want to solve your problems!"; "We want to offer integrated solutions!") and of course these themes weren't always consistent. The result was confusion inside and outside the company; there was no unanimity in the approach to customers.

The group didn't have the ultimate say as to what the message should be, but they fully understood the importance of having one unifying message to which all other company messages could be linked. They believed they had the potential to take the lead in seeing that a message was created and established.

I had little to offer except my belief that the problem was solvable and with less effort than they imagined, if I, as well as they, would take a risk. I was clear on this. Risk is often involved when people are in the process of change. I told myself that I trusted myself to wade into these unknown waters, and support myself and the group for learning. I continued on, inventing the process as I went forward, feeling somehow supported and not alone, trusting that whatever happened, it would be fine.

I asked the group to let me take them on a thought journey and they agreed with some questioning sideways glances. We were in a business meeting, so it was risky to ask the group members to close their eyes, as I did, but to make it safer for myself, I told myself that we were all "just learning." The warm-up exercises had paved the way and they agreed to participate. They shut their eyes.

I proposed that they imagine that each of them was on an island. It was a beautiful, warm sunny day—the temperature was perfect for a relaxed stroll on the beach. I told them they had nowhere to go, no work to do—they were there simply to explore. I told them to picture themselves walking on the beach, toes in the soft white sand, with birds singing overhead, everywhere the smell of the sea, the sound of waves crashing—it was an idyllic setting.

I then had them imagine that up ahead they saw an object in the sand and that it drew their curiosity. As they approached, they could see that the object was in fact a beautiful treasure chest, very ornate, with an open lock. I told them that it had been left there especially for them to open. Then each person was to open the chest and discover the treasure that had been left in it for them, and that they would know, instantly, the significance of the gift— what it meant and why it had been left for them to find. After giving them some time, I asked them to come back in the room and told them to open their eyes.

I then went around the room asking each person to share what his or her gift had been and its significance. As they did, I listed the gifts on a flip chart along with a couple of words about what the gift meant to them.

One person said, "The chest was empty, and I realized suddenly that *I* was the gift. I have all that I need to be of great service in the world. This was a wonderful discovery and I felt a great peace in understanding the message."

Another said, "In my chest there was a giant book with answers to all the questions ever asked. I realized that the book was me, our group, and our company, and that we simply need to answer the questions that we're asked. I don't know why, but it feels like a big burden has been lifted. Now I know what to do."

As each person shared, there was a warmth and peaceful sense of surrender in the room. No one was trying to accomplish anything. Each person was exploring inwardly the wisdom they had brought forward. It was wonderful to experience.

When everyone had revealed the nature of their gift and explored its meaning, I said to them, "Take a moment to look over the words and phrases on the flip chart."

We switched gears slightly. I reminded them of the problem they had posed earlier, which had been set aside. I then asked, "What do these words and phrases have in common? How do they relate to the problem you're trying to solve, about your fundamental message to customers? What do these words suggest the company message should be? If the treasures left for you were no accident, but instead were intended to guide you to a solution, and if each of you held a part of the solution, what would the solution be?"

The group studied the list for a couple of minutes then slowly, but with accelerating speed, started calling out ideas and suggestions. Suddenly, the ideas coalesced into a single idea shared by everyone in the room: *How can we be of service?*

Was this the message we were after? What if every company communication, brochure, sales call, product promotion, and strategy, every new product had the "How can we be of service?" message behind it? That would make for a highly service-oriented relationship by which the company sought to understand customer needs, match them with its products and services and meet their needs with value offerings. As a customer, I would be delighted to be approached that way. Fewer than ten

words. It fit who the company was, what it was about. It was recognizable as an implicit "philosophy" already in place at the company, just never formally expressed.

It was an extraordinary moment for everyone in the group—it felt like we were riding a wave of creativity. And finding the theme had taken less than an hour.

We quickly outlined a plan for talking with others about the idea, reminding ourselves that even if the message didn't turn out to be the exact one the company ended up with, it was an illustration of what had been missing—a single customer-intention that everyone could keep in mind, and that would serve to unify the approach to customers.

The implications of having such a message were huge. The group began to appreciate how, using it, the content of all communication with customers would change for the better. Instead of encouraging customers to want the products, as another phrase might, this message focused on what the company might do for the customer, how the product served the customer's needs. A unifying intention like this would make a powerful difference in terms of aligning the creativity of employees to customer service versus customer manipulation.

> **Suddenly, the ideas coalesced into a single idea shared by everyone in the room:** *How can we be of service?*

As the discussion wound down, I noticed the drooping shoulders of one individual. He no longer seemed excited. What was going on? I looked around the room; everyone seemed to be in a similar state. The exhilaration had gone and something else had taken its place. Something that felt heavy.

Trying to get at what had happened, I asked the group to talk about what fears and concerns they had about going forward.

Dan, the person with the drooping shoulders, spoke first. "I somehow think that we can't pull it off, getting the message accepted," he said. "I imagine that we'll be navigating heavy political waters around here, we'll encounter resistance, and the whole thing will just collapse and come to nothing."

Good, I thought—he's being open about his fears. The first step to getting to the heart of anything is to take off the outside layer and Dan had just done that.

"And if that happens," I said softly, "if it comes to nothing and you're not successful, what will you conclude about yourself? You, personally."

He went right to the core of his fear. "That I just don't have what it takes," he said. "That I'm not good enough."

Dan went further, explaining how this pattern was nothing new. "That's what always happens to me," he said. "I take something on, it doesn't work out, and I decide I just don't have what it takes, that I'm not good enough."

Our eyes met and I saw him suddenly as a child, looking up, wanting to do well, but getting the message that what he did, whatever it was, wasn't good enough—that *he* wasn't good enough. And then I saw the years pile on him, years of collecting evidence that this belief was true. Without words, I let him know I understood, knew how painful the fear of inadequacy was for him.

Other beliefs like Dan's surfaced in the room, though none expressed so gracefully as he had done. Then I challenged the group: "What if this whole project—your frustration at the lack of a core message to customers, your coming here and getting aligned to the message as easily as you did—is all about coming to terms with the bigger issues you face in your lives? What if understanding the nature of those issues is the real challenge you confront each day, and that the tasks you face at work are designed to assist you in meeting those inner challenges? What if the purpose of the outer challenge is to assist and support you in resolving an inner dilemma?"

Now this was thinking outside the box! What I was asking the group to consider was a paradigm shift in its belief structure from conventional to unconventional beliefs. In the conventional belief model, we imagine that our talents and experiences give us the opportunity to solve important problems or accomplish certain tasks. If we are not successful at these things, we at least gain more experience and will, hopefully, be more successful the next time. When we are successful, we feel good about who we are; we feel we can be given even greater challenges, which we can meet successfully, and finally be the person we want to be.

But what if it works differently? What if this model works to a point, but something else is happening on a deeper level? What if the challenges, the "successes" we have, the lessons learned, are actually designed to reveal what and who we truly are? What if they are designed to provide us the opportunity to express our full creativity, passions, and talents in a way that is aligned with a unique purpose for us on the planet, a purpose that is also embedded in our hearts? What if discovering our belief limitations, and healing them, is the key to accelerating our productivity, achieving our goals and fulfilling our purpose?

And what if every project we're engaged in gives us the chance to do this—and is, in fact, the point of any challenge we face? If we accept these beliefs, assuming from the start that we have nothing to prove and everything to learn, then life on the job becomes a much different path.

I concluded by reminding the group that I wasn't asking them to believe all this because I was saying it, but to consider how effective they might be if they choose to hold these beliefs. In other words, I asked them to consider if adopting these beliefs would assist them in reaching goals more easily.

I don't remember planning to say these words. The inspiration, the way the ideas had unfolded throughout the day, felt like divine guidance. The group understood what I was saying, considered it, and considered the broader implications as well.

What had brought this leap in success with the group was trust. I had had an idea of how to link outward challenges with inward dilemmas but had been fearful of com-

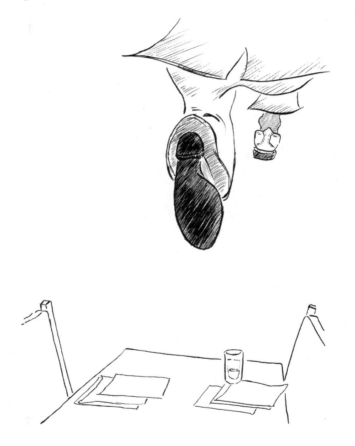

municating it, held back by the concern that I wouldn't do it right. And I had historical data to suggest that when I went "too far" the results weren't always good.

But there was a difference here. I wasn't coming from

arrogance or blind zeal, but from a willingness to do my best, to learn and to be of service to others. When I became willing to risk putting my ideas to work, to learn and discover and take risks in the process, I healed my own limiting belief, a fear. And by doing that, I was able to find out more about who I am and to be that person—and to learn how to serve others in the process. So by trusting myself to show up and do my best—by letting go of the expectation that I needed to do it "right" and "good"—grace and ease had shown up in the meeting rather than a "hole in the road."

> So by trusting myself to show up and do my best, grace and ease had shown up in the meeting rather than a "hole in the road."

Dan approached me later on. "But how do I address the issue I have about being good enough?" he asked. "How do I get past that so I don't keep running into the same trouble on every project that I do?" He was looking at me intently, with open determination.

"Good question," I answered, "and asking that question is a good place to start." I then told him about the executive development program we offer, which is designed to support people like Dan in situations like the one he was in. I said that the issues he was talking about were not necessarily easy to deal with (although they might be), but that having a one-on-one coach to help him through the process was one way to approach it. I told him he was holding beliefs about himself that were limiting his ability to accomplish what he wanted to; that by acting as if these beliefs were true, he had made them so. I described a process by which he would explore how his beliefs were formed in order to "heal their memory" and let them go.

Dan entered the coaching program a couple of months later. His objectives were to let go of blaming others for his failures and to assume one-hundred percent responsibility for his success; to disconnect his sense of self-worth from what he did or did not achieve in favor of having the freedom to learn and keep learning how to be more and more successful.

Dan began to see that the core of his dilemma had to do with his mental habit of seeing every boss in a paternal role, as a harsh critic. Fundamentally, he felt himself a victim in such relationships, powerless and unable to fight back effectively, getting only so far and then deciding that no matter what, the "parent" wasn't going to change, and his only option was to give up.

This victim pattern is tough because it presupposes that someone has to be powerless. From the point of view of the "victim," it's impossible to come out on top unless you overpower the person with authority, in effect, making them the victim. (If I have the world organized in this fashion—divided into victims and victimizers—I have to be one or the other in every situation I find myself in. This is a particularly challenging version of the right-wrong model because if I'm "right," I am still "wronged.")

Dan had a gift in his ability to perceive and understand his feelings and those of others, and to empathize with others. In the business world of which I've been a part, this is an unusual gift. In discussing projects that involved other people, he had a sense of their concerns, an understanding of what their resistance was about and how to address it. He also had the courage to step forward and express his feelings—how, for example, he felt when he would start talking and someone in the room would interrupt him to tell him he didn't have the necessary experience to understand a situation. And at times like that, all he wanted to do was leave the room, the project, the company—to quit.

When Dan began to open up more and express himself when these situations occurred, he found himself becoming more productive. As Dan became more aware of his unique skills and the value of them, he became more confident in bringing his skills forward, and this had a positive effect on those with whom he worked. His skill in talking about his emotions brought greater awareness to others about the way simple acts of disrespect could impact negatively on productivity. His colleagues at work began to understand that they shared Dan's feelings, even if they didn't have the skill to express them clearly, and began to appreciate their subtle influence. They saw that they could learn something from Dan.

Because Dan had skills in emotional awareness, he could understand his boss's feelings when at one point his boss expressed frustration about Dan's handling of data. Dan could empathize with his boss's point of view and let the immediate emotion he experienced go by, focusing instead on the information conveyed that he could use. "Data and numbers and analysis have been a challenge for me," Dan told his boss, "but I think I'm ready to address it. Who do you think I could work with around here who would be willing to show me how to do that?" Over time, his skill at receiving feedback effectively influenced others and caused the flow of feedback in the department to increase.

Still, there were problems. About half-way into the program, Dan's coach talked with me about his progress. "He's still having a hard time letting go of blaming the company and his boss for anything bad that happens to him. He may end up leaving the company and the coaching program and taking the issue with him. He's very frustrated and angry, but I don't see him moving past blaming others yet for those feelings. He doesn't want to let go of that point of view."

Several weeks later, about ninety percent of the way through the program, Dan put the coaching sessions on hold. Quitting was his pattern and it had shown up again; the underlying belief that Dan couldn't come to terms with—I can't be successful until my "parent" changes, and if I can't get him to do that, I quit—had reasserted its hold in the sessions themselves.

No matter what our skills and competencies are, or how much we have achieved, when we encounter the area of a blind spot, a core fear, we can become quite incapacitated. If Dan stopped blaming others for his lack of success, he would have to consider that maybe he was responsible for his own "failure." And he might feel in the process that his greatest fear, that he didn't have what it takes, was "true." The more Dan fears that this is the case, the greater his need to protect himself. Being a victim was the way Dan made life "safe" for himself—our blind spots exist to protect us from seeing what appears true and is painful to acknowledge. What Dan would need to see was that he was simply learning how to go to the next level in all he does.

From the perspective that the *real* goal is to recognize and heal our blind spots so we can be who we are, we draw situations to ourselves that represent what we must heal to be who we truly are. In Dan's case, what was in the way of his making additional emotional progress, what had to be healed, was his misperception of not being good enough. When Dan realizes that the issue of his being good enough was determined long before he could walk, talk or deliver astute analysis, he'll be able to disconnect worthiness from accomplishment. He'll be free to accomplish what he can because life will no longer be about proving that he's good enough to be worth caring about. He won't have to be a victim, he'll be free to experiment with and explore his talent. Until then, he can expect to continue to attract "proofs" of his fear of unworthiness and blame others for it, until his pain becomes so great he becomes willing to face his fear head on.

When we let go of blaming and go instead for learning, then actual learning starts. Dan wasn't ready to do this, his fear was too great, so his progress was interrupted. It will take Dan whatever time it takes for him to shift from blaming to learning.

I can say this now, but on the day I learned about his decision to put the coaching program on hold, this wasn't so clear. At the time, I felt a too-familiar panic at the prospect that we had failed, failed with Dan. What if our program was blamed, declared not good enough? What if negative word spread and our rapidly growing program in this organization started to dwindle in attendance? And what if it *were* all true—that the program *wasn't* good enough—that *I* wasn't good enough.

And then I forgave myself for the negative judgment that my own worthiness required "proof": I didn't need to base my sense of self-worth on whether people remained in the program or not, I told myself. Instead, I surrendered to the ongoing process of learning.

And in doing so, I was able to consider what there was to learn from this experience. Maybe, in regard to the coaching program, we needed to look at the up-front part of it and review how we structure individual commitment to the process to determine how best to support people who want to quit. That was helpful to consider.

It's always useful to recognize core fears; but even when we recognize them, they may not fully retreat from our experience—at least mine haven't yet. Once we know what they are, however, we can begin to recognize them at an ever-faster rate—minutes instead of months. And once we recognize what is happening—when we see we are out of balance and upset and blaming others—we can learn how to support ourselves better, thereby returning ourselves to a productive state with greater ease.

For me, this is a matter of forgiving myself for judging myself unworthy, or judging myself worthy on the condition of accomplishment. I make it okay with myself to be still learning. I make it okay for me to take the time it takes to learn what I need to know, and this makes it easier for me to be gentle with others, like Dan, about the time it takes for them to learn.

And when I remind myself of these truths, I come back into balance. From the learning perspective I simply have curiosity—and less anger, frustration, upset, or annoyance. Instead I experience a desire to keep investigating, gratitude for the opportunities to do so, and a wish to continue to assist others on their journey toward their full potential.

In this process, I have still encountered the fear that surfaces when I wonder whether I have what it takes—whether I am "good enough." I know these are tests, designed to assist me in revealing a different slant on the self-judgment. But I am seeing, and addressing, these instances of lack of faith in myself more quickly. I am learning from them and staying more productive more of the time with each new learning. I believe, because it supports me to do so, that I will look back and notice that the test has disappeared, that this hole in the road is gone, and then I will know that I have learned what I was being given the opportunity to learn.

‡ ‡ ‡

Recently I conducted a program for a new client where I had the experience of walking down a familiar path, where formerly there had been a hole, but which was there no longer.

I was facilitating a day-long dialogue discussion between operations and sales in a large service business whose clients are large corporations. The president of the company was there, along with about a dozen individuals from both organizations. The challenge was one I had come across before—sales, responding to pressure from customers, promised short timelines and innovative "bells and whistles" without appreciating what it would take to execute the deliverables. Operations wanted to be heard and to have their advice taken seriously so that programs would be implemented effectively and customer satisfaction would be increased. Sales wanted operations to be

> **A common goal is the basis for resolving conflicts.**

more flexible because they felt pressure to meet aggressive growth targets, and customers were not always willing to follow the internal standard of how long it took to implement programs.

While a myriad of detailed issues and process changes needed to be addressed, we started with identifying the common goal between operations and sales. A common goal is the basis for resolving conflicts like this, rather than a debate about who is right. Issues can then be addressed in the context of "What will enable *us* to move effectively toward *our* goal?"

To build the case for needing a common goal, I asked the group to stand in a circle and, one after another, to throw a ball of yarn from person to person. As they tossed the yarn, I had them complete these phrases, with the intention of encouraging an expression of mutual interdependency and respect: "The way my success depends upon you is . . . " and "One talent you bring to the table in that regard is . . . ".

The most common individual refrain, after hearing how someone felt about them, was "I didn't know that . . . that's a surprise!"

When we were done, everyone had been linked, clearly establishing that success for each person depended on every other person in the room. They also saw that for the group to be successful, they needed a shared goal.

One person offered: "Our goal is simple: meet customer requests at any cost."

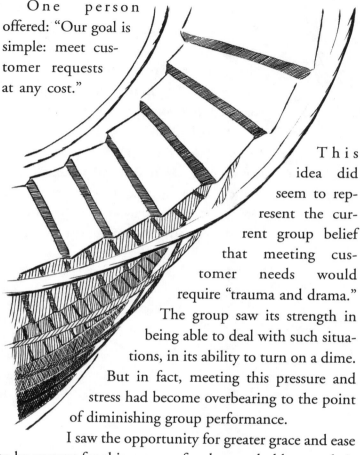

This idea did seem to represent the current group belief that meeting customer needs would require "trauma and drama." The group saw its strength in being able to deal with such situations, in its ability to turn on a dime. But in fact, meeting this pressure and stress had become overbearing to the point of diminishing group performance.

I saw the opportunity for greater grace and ease to be present for this group—for them to hold on to their strength of "changing on a dime," but to raise productivity by finding ways to eliminate unnecessary work that occurred when the group became too involved in its culture of "can-do."

I made this suggestion: what if you change your belief about who you are from "We please customers no matter what the cost" to "We please customers with grace and ease." I spoke momentarily about the power of belief

> **I realized the concept of greater grace and ease had taken hold within me.**

structures but I saw that the group was right there with me, nodding their heads, appreciating the concept, talking about what a difference that would make. They understood. And in the detailed work that followed, this concept of greater grace and ease started to take hold in them. It was powerful. And I realized that the concept of greater grace and ease had taken more hold within me. I was no longer presuming that a conversation about belief structures would be difficult. And this was making it possible to assist others toward their goals with accelerated speed.

Going, Going, GONG

How disappointments and disapproval can yield intuition and wisdom

▼

Words can communicate
the experience to somebody
who already has had it or
is right on the verge of it.
But not to somebody
who does not know.

—

A. H. ALMAAS

CHAPTER 7

Going, Going, GONG

SOME will remember a 70's television favorite, "The Gong Show." Contestants were given a few minutes to perform on stage in any way they chose. The audience responded to their acts showing either approval or disapproval. If there was booing or hissing, the emcee would take a giant hammer-like club and strike a huge gong, the loud G-O-N-G letting the performer know in no uncertain terms that it was time to quit. The goal was to perform for the full time allowed without getting gonged.

For me life has sometimes felt like this—as if I'm trying to avoid getting "gonged." The gongs represent "no" messages, sometimes sent directly, as in "you're fired," and sometimes sent subtly as a signal of disappointment or disapproval. Concern about disappointing others or being disapproved of by them made it challenging to learn to trust my instincts. I might think I had a good idea, but what would others say?

Learning to distinguish between my intuitive ideas about how to go forward, and the doubts that hold me back because I fear disapproval, has been pivotal for me. Developing and trusting my intuitive skills avails me of wisdom that has made solving problems and accomplishing tasks much easier, and has added innovation, creativity and depth to my problem-solving strategies.

This journey took time and involved a paradigm shift, a new interpretation of what that G-O-N-G meant. It required learning to see what seemed like a gong, not as a bad thing, but as a kind of lighthouse showing me a safe way into the harbor of my intuition. It also required letting go of the myth that I was on my own.

I have always had a fairly inventive imagination when it comes to problem solving. Perhaps this was seeded at an early age. As a youth I spent most of my time in our Oregon farm fields. I didn't so much mind the work—but my mind would wander and I would try to invent ways of getting it done other than, say, leaning over a row of berries from dawn until late afternoon. I rarely bothered to mention these ideas—I learned quickly that my ideas seemed too far-out and weren't paid attention to.

This interest in discovering new ways of doing work carried over into business. My career started in the transportation industry where I was fascinated by the flow of raw materials and finished products that most companies were engaged in managing. Early on, I discovered that about twenty-five percent of our gross national product is directly related to managing these flows, and most of what businesses do indirectly affects them. This was major! I often let my mind wander, trying to figure out a better way to manage these flows. I had read about business legends—individuals who had changed the course of the world with their inventions, their ability to see new ways of doing things. I thought my future—and the recognition of my worth—lay in inventing some amazing concept that would revolutionize business.

Back in the 80's when I was cutting my teeth in the railroad industry, I saw a different way to operate a part of the railroad's train service. In those days, railroad cars were either operated in unit trains (a group of about a hundred cars traveling together conveying a single commodity) or in regular, single railcar service. To have access to a unit train, you had to have huge volumes to ship—a hundred cars of grain, for example, all going to the same destination. These trains moved nonstop in dedicated service as a unit from where they originated to their destinations, and service was pretty good. With the usual service, it might take thirty days for a rail car to travel from the Midwest to the Gulf. The rail car would travel a hundred miles or so and then enter a yard where all the cars would have to be mechanically switched from one train to another. Some cars would languish in yards for several days waiting for room on an available outbound train to the appropriate destination. It was slow going.

The idea I had come up with was "book trains," ten cars that would be identified as linked together but move in regular service. The ten cars would be switched as a unit, saving time and the associated operating costs. Book train units would be flagged, switched first, and moved out on the first available train. We estimated that it would reduce travel time of a given rail trip by two-thirds. This was a big plus because in those days shortages of rail cars for carrying grain were rampant. Return on assets would skyrocket. The concept was adopted by the railroad and the trains went into service.

The shippers naturally loved the idea and quickly booked the available book trains. The train crews who operated the switching yards resisted initially—it was just one more thing to deal with, they felt—but they went along as I visited the various yards and talked the concept over with them. My farm training came in handy—I respected people who labored outdoors all day because I knew what that entailed and the satisfaction that came from it. The rail-yard managers didn't receive that many personal visits from people at headquarters, and certainly not from young women with big dreams, and we developed an easy rapport whereby they would help me out by moving the book trains along.

One shipper exceeded the strict time limits for loading cars and screamed bloody murder when his book train was taken away and given to a competitor, but the operations vice president held the line with me asserting that if we were going to make this unique concept work, then everyone had to play by the rules.

> The conclusion I drew was that my idea had been a good one, but there were greater forces at play. It was a gong.

We were creating real momentum with this concept when the railroad's financial performance floundered beyond recovery and the company went bankrupt. The conclusion I drew was that my idea had been a good one, but there were greater forces at play than I could address. It was a gong, but one not in my control—akin to appearing on the gong show when another contestant had the advantage because a hundred of their relatives were in the audience. "I was a good inventor, but,

darn, just not in the
right place at the right
time," I told myself.

In my eagerness to
claim sole credit for
the idea, I had, how-
ever, forgotten some-
thing important about
the way innovation
works. I had forgotten
that the head of oper-
ations had worked

with me to think through and sell the idea to management; that the yard managers had figured out a way to
make it work on a practical level; and that many others
had to come together to experiment with a new idea.

In the mid 80's, while working for another company,
I wrote a paper about how "outsourcing" certain back-
room functions—farming out administrative processes
like arranging for product transportation—might become
a profitable business. It made sense in terms of what was
happening to the infrastructure of technology. If a given
function was not part of a company's core strength, then
why should it invest money to build information systems
and hire people with expertise in a particular area to try to
handle that function as well as their competitors might?
Maybe the company would be better served by outsourcing the function to an organization that had already
invested substantial resources in the area, and focus its
limited resources on further developing its own core
strengths.

In particular, I was looking at my company's ability to manage assets and operations in the logistics area. I postulated that it might be possible for my company to take over these functions for major companies like Xerox and Ford, and thus create a profitable, new business opportunity. Companies like Xerox and Ford had internal organizations that managed logistics, but new systems were being invented that could handle these freight flows more effectively. It didn't make sense for every company to invest in these systems when there were other demands for limited capital resources that were more related to core competencies. I called the concept the third-party logistics outsourcing opportunity. While this terminology is commonplace today, in those days, it was a confusing mouthful of concepts.

In fact, it was a radical idea at the time. And the reaction of my company was that no large firm would consider outsourcing key functions to a third-party because it would make them dependent on that company and therefore not in control of their own future.

I took this reaction as a gong. My interpretation was that I hadn't the internal clout to demand the kind of attention needed so that my ideas could, at the very least, be fully considered. It was disappointing, but I let the

matter drop. In claiming the idea as mine, I had neglect-
ed to fully recognize the group of industry-thinkers who
were also aware of this new business trend, and whose
thinking helped shape my own.

When I left the company, others started pursuing the
idea I had championed, turning it into
nearly a billion dollar opportunity in ten
years, to my amazement. No one remembered where the idea had "originated." I
took this as another gong, a verification of
my initial interpretation that I lacked the
clout to be fully "heard." In doing so, I discounted the talent and stamina and operational fortitude that it had
taken to bring the idea to fruition. To me, "they" had ben-
efited from *my* creativity without so much as a thank you.
Major G-O-N-G.

> I see that my focus was on my being the idea's source.

I now see that my focus at the time was on whether
my creative ideas were well-received, that is, on the reactions of others to me, and on my being the idea's source. I
was involved with the impact the idea had on the world,
which I saw as a measure of its value, and therefore of
mine.

Feedback is important. But defining the value of an
idea based upon the opinions of others is a trap. We can
only be as creative as others "allow" us to be. We stop experiencing our own value and give the power to determine it
to others. We aren't free to create.

And there's an even bigger trap: the presumption that
intuition, creativity, inventiveness somehow reside solely
within us. Anyone who has ever worked in an organization
appreciates that there is no such thing as one person's idea.

And even this notion—that we are all constantly influencing one another's creativity—considers only a small part of the creative energy available to us. When we are ready, we begin to understand that there is a universal source of creativity that we can tap into if we wish. As we see this, the door opens to the possibility of accessing creativity and intuition on a whole new level.

> Once we make this switch, it's like we're being gonged once and for all, but this time in enlightenment.

In my case, disconnecting the creative experience and the value it produces from my value as a person was the first step in proactively assessing this universal creativity. Understanding that I was worthy of recognition, whether or not I was being appreciated, was an essential step that freed me to access creativity. Instead of being creative to get something (recognition), I could be creative just because I was.

Our intuitiveness, creativity, and inventiveness are gifts. It makes a difference whether we tap into these gifts with joy and in service to others, or to demonstrate our worth, which we don't need to do. The worthiness of an individual simply is—it's not something that requires proof through demonstration. It's good fortune when we allow the gongs in life to guide us more steadily along the path of discovering the source of multi-dimensional creative intuition.

Once we make this switch, it's like we're being gonged once and for all, but this time in enlightenment. And once that happens, there's no turning back. Life and our approach to it changes. We become much more willing to consider new possibilities. We learn to develop and trust inner wisdom as a guide to self-expression, as a guide to how we operate in the world. We realize that staying in alignment with our wisdom is much more important than focusing on the opinions of others.

Oddly, when this happened to me, I began to value what others had to say

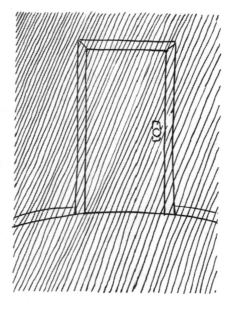

more because I valued the essence of who they were. I began to listen out of respect regardless of whether my experiences matched theirs or whether I had a similar perspective. Developing this inner core of wisdom seemed to open a channel for developing my intuition. The more I accessed my inner wisdom, the more I came to trust what I heard inwardly.

As I attuned to what different experiences told me, I concluded that my experiences were not fully random. I began to feel as if people, circumstances and experiences that were on my path represented what was most important for me to learn. It seemed as though I had assistance in this. From this perspective, it was only a small step, albeit a leap of faith, for me to begin to engage more directly with the "source" of this assistance. This is not to advocate any particular religious orientation, only to say that when I acted as if assistance was available, things seemed to unfold with grace and ease.

I vividly recall the first time I consciously tapped into a source outside myself to stimulate my intuition and creativity during a business meeting. It was like the first time I put on glasses; I realized how much of what was available to see I had been missing.

IT'S IN EVERY ONE OF US

It's in Every One of Us to be wise
Find your heart and open up both your eyes
We can all know everything without
*   ever knowing why*
It's in Every One of Us by and by...

— DAVID POMERANTZ

I was involved in a two-day process with a CEO and his team, assisting them in wresting with a strategic decision. The specifics of the debate were old news to them. The group had broken into two evenly divided camps who had become weary with the repetition of arguments. I got that there wasn't much listening going on. The CEO was unwilling to step into one camp at the risk of alienating the other camp. It was a standoff.

I felt stuck, too. I had tried a number of ideas for breaking through the impasse without success. I needed a new idea.

I had been flirting with the idea of intuition, what it was, how to develop it, and I had reached the point of considering that there was a creative consciousness available to all of us if we simply knew how to tap into it. To do this meant, I saw, that I would have to give up the idea that any creative idea I had was mine alone. I wanted to help this group, but it felt like a risk to invoke intuition in a business meeting. What if it didn't work? What if they rolled their eyes and laughed? But I had run out of options, and I was willing to take the risk.

On a break, I said to myself, okay, I'm now making a request to the creative consciousness. I need an idea that will work here.

And before my thought was completed, the idea of what to do was there in front of me. It came partially in words, partially as an image and partially as a sensation; and at the same time it was a knowing beyond the senses. Yet, my understanding of the idea was crystal clear. I was to put the two camps in separate rooms and have each of them come up with ten reasons why the other camp's idea might be right.

My first reaction to this idea was fear-based and negative. 'They'll never do it,' I thought. This was a conservative company, not into relationship-building exercises. All of the participants except one were men, and they were all older than I was, which made me wary of their willingness to do what I told them to do. I was afraid if I asked them to follow my idea they would reject it and then where would I be?

I decided I needed clarification, so I asked the creative consciousness, "Are you sure?"

"Do it," was what I got back.

And so I did, getting the group quickly into the two

rooms before they could organize a "no," then giving them clear instructions to report back in twenty minutes with their lists. Then I walked out before there could be any questions. My knees were wobbling, but to my amazement, they followed my instructions.

The impact of the exercise was dramatic. Suddenly the atmosphere of conflict lifted. The group began to hear and see one another's positions and to consider the validity and value in all perspectives. They quickly found a middle path. Moreover, the CEO became much more effective, as he no longer felt he had to pick one side over the other; instead, he charted a course forward.

Now, what I had the group do was not something never before tried on the planet. It was, however, an idea that *I* had never tried before, one that I had recognized because I got willing to trust my intuition and experiment with a creative solution. I had also recognized, as a "by-product" of that trust, that I didn't feel alone in my task. I felt safer than I typically had in facilitating meetings, and more supported.

> I continued to experiment with my partner-in-intuition, the creative consciousness.

I continued to experiment with my partner-in-intuition, the creative consciousness. In one instance, prior to working with a team off-site for a few days, I went into an art supply store in a state just above sleep-walking and put items in my shopping cart that my intuition directed me to buy. I had no idea what I would use these for. But the "off-site" unfolded in dramatic ways I couldn't have anticipated and the items turned out to be a perfect "fit" for problem solving.

At another time I consciously tapped into the creative consciousness when I found myself meeting with the operating crew of a fabric dye house. I had been meeting with the company's CEO and new owner about challenges he was facing as he took over the helm of the company. Most of the dye house work-

ers and their leaders had worked for the company for near-ly forty years. They had their way of doing things.

The CEO knew the employees were not expressing themselves openly with him. He was frustrated; on the one hand, he wanted them to try some of his new ideas. On the other, he wanted to consider their concerns and feedback. He hoped I could assist in getting some honest conversation started. But, he wondered, would they open up to me?

During this discussion, on impulse, he got on the intercom and asked seven or eight people to come into the conference room. As they were entering he told me, "Let's see if they will open up to you."

He introduced me by name and said he wanted the group to talk with me; then he left. Clearly, none of us

were expecting this. I knew they had work to do. I silently put it to the creative consciousness: "So, what do we do
here?"

"Just love them." was the response. I was so into trusting my intuition at that point, I didn't even consider that
this thought was anything but totally reasonable. I looked
around the room at each of them, and considered their
essential nature, loving what I saw. It took a few seconds
and it relaxed me enormously. I felt no need to control the
situation and make it come out right. They were more
important than the outcome.

Then I told them the truth: the CEO thought com-
munications could work better, and the CEO was considering hiring me to help him with that. But, I told
them, I was only going to be able to help if they were willing to trust me and talk with me about their feelings and
on-the-job experiences. One by one, they started sharing,
first complaining, but then under gentle nudges exploring how their personal fears and concerns were getting
triggered by their boss's personality. It was one of the
most heartfelt discussions I had ever had. The CEO called
me the next day. "I don't know what you did to them," he
said, "but they said that whatever I was paying you, it
wasn't enough."

For another client, I was planning a concluding meeting where thirty-five participants would gather to celebrate the success of a project. I wanted to give them amus-
ing and yet meaningful tokens of the group's spirit that
they could take home as reminders of what they had
accomplished. I didn't have much time to think about
this, but it had gotten so that I didn't need it; my co-cre-

ator, creative consciousness, was very reliable. So I set a bedtime intention. I asked the creative consciousness for ideas to be present when I awoke. And the next morning, they were there, absolutely appropriate items laid out in my mind's eye, in color, complete and perfect.

I know that I have a lot of company in experimenting with intuition. Once, while conducting a leadership seminar with a segment on intuition, the manager of production suddenly perked up. "I use intuition all the time," he said. "But I never knew that anyone else did. I've never heard anyone talk about it. It's like a picture floats in front of me of some way to improve the operations or manufacturing line. It just appears, and I get this calm, peaceful feeling, and I know to draw my vision on a sheet of paper. Intuition is how I get some of my best ideas."

Here's how I experience accessing intuition in myself: I center myself in my essential core, where my values lie, in the source of my heart energy, at the level of the soul, where I find my wisdom and my knowing; then, I become aware of a connection to all that has been and will be in consciousness, a connection to and with a higher consciousness. And in this place I trust Spirit and what comes forward.

I have also heard people say that the five senses developed at different times and we are in the midst of evolving a sixth sense, that of intuition. This also resonates with me. However, intellectual explanations somehow seem limiting. What seems more productive is to explore and learn.

As I explore the path of multi-sensory creative intuition (that is, a knowing beyond the five senses' way of knowing) I have learned to remind myself of three things.

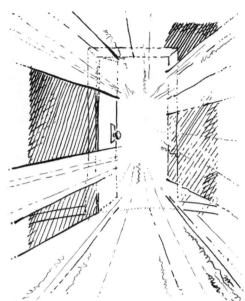

The first is to keep my ego in check; I remind myself that, whatever discoveries I make, they are not about me or my intuition. I've discovered that when I make it about me, I trip over my own two feet. For example, one time I went into a Chinese open-air market and bought fifteen masks, convinced that I had had an intuitive "hit" to do this. At the time I was attached to getting intuitive hits and I wanted a big one to demonstrate my intuitive power. I still have the masks in a box, gathering dust. They remind me of the many faces and pitfalls of an ego-based search for intuition—of being attached to being intuitive as an indicator of worthiness.

The second reminder I keep close to my awareness in pursuing intuition is that I need to come from a place of wanting to be of service. I don't have to know how I am serving others, but if my intention is to be in service, then whatever happens will be fine.

The desire to be of service emerges when we seek our unique reason for being, our purpose; an intention of wanting to be of service doesn't preclude personal gain. It is simply an internal orientation. In a given situation, we don't seek to win or get what we want, but to use our gifts, talents and creativity in service to others. As we become attuned to our purpose and are clear about wanting to act in alignment with our unique destiny, a wish to be of service springs forward as naturally as breathing.

> **As we become attuned, a wish to be of service springs forward naturally.**

The third reminder is that if I am feeling fear or any strong negative emotion, then what is going on probably has very little to do with intuition. I have learned that the part of me through which I access intuition is not the same part of me that is speaking when a fearful/negative future fantasy is present. So if I'm fearful about what may happen, something other than my intuition is probably engaged.

On the other hand, if I have an intuition, and at the same time I notice no attachment to whether it's accurate or not, that I'm emotionally "clear," then my intuition is highly reliable.

I've also noticed that as I work, the process of using my emotions to reveal areas about which I've harshly judged myself, accompanied by self-forgiveness for these self-judgments, allows me greater access to my creative intuitive nature. And with greater access to it, my intuition has strengthened.

This doesn't mean that I always operate fully attuned to my intuition. Staying in balance—staying clear—has been a challenge for me. Rather than be disappointed about this, however, I have come to celebrate the gift that learning opportunities represent.

One such learning experience occurred not so

long ago. I was returning home on a flight from Texas. As the plane landed and I stood to gather my belongings, I saw a senior executive with whom I'd worked sitting a few rows back. I considered just walking off the plane without speaking with him. It had been a long couple of days and while he and I had done business a number of times, it could not be said that we were friends. But I had often wished we could be on more trusting terms, so I decided to catch his attention and walk with him to the baggage claim.

We said hi and stepped on the escalator. Harry's first question to me seemed pointed. "Who are you working for at the company these days?" he asked, a reference to the fact that we continued to do business with his organization. I recalled hearing a couple of years earlier that Harry had made a case that my firm was doing too much work for his company and that maybe it wouldn't be such a good thing to use us so much. I had been wary since then because asking me who I was working for always seemed to be his first or second question.

I hedged, not really revealing anything, just nodding slightly, adjusting my grip on my bags. He no doubt noticed my discomfort, which probably made him want to know all the more. He restated the question in a way that said, I am going to keep asking until you answer.

I took a gulp and tried to appear nonchalant. "Well there is that one project I told you about the last time we talked. That's still going on. And then I'm also working with Sara here and there," I said, mentioning the name of an executive at the company.

He looked grave. Then he said emphatically, with a bit of tension in his voice, "You two sure have a weird relationship."

What a strange comment, I thought to myself. "Well, I don't think it's weird at all," I said. "I like Sara."

"Well when I talk to Sara," Harry continued, "she always says that she isn't going to use you anymore and then the next thing you know, she calls you for another assignment."

I was stunned. Why would he tell me this? If it were true, I would certainly be disappointed. Sara and I talked often about how we valued our relationship because we could be open when one of us was upset with the other. It would have disappointed me if Sara had been upset and hadn't been willing to share that fact with me. But whether it was true or not, why would he be repeating such a comment?

I puzzled over this on the drive home. I thought I would call Sara the next day and mention the conversation. It seemed like it couldn't go unaddressed. But I didn't need to as Sara called me first thing next morning.

"Hey," she said, "I wanted to talk with you. Harry came by my office this morning and said he had run into you at the airport. He told me what he had said to you. And I asked him why would you tell her that? I have to tell you, I don't know what he was talking about or what possessed him to say that. But this is a good thing. It may help you understand what I mean when I say people around here don't always tell the truth."

"I'm glad you called," I said. "It was pretty weird. He must have been feeling funny about having made it to drop by your office first thing to tell you we had met. I mean I'm thinking to myself, even if it is true, why would he say it?"

"That's right," she said. "And even if it were true, why would he tell you?" We confirmed our agreement to talk as planned the following week and said goodbye.

But it wasn't done for me. I found myself stuck on the encounter, replaying it in my mind, looking for a clue to its meaning that I might have missed. There must have been *some* truth in what Harry said, I told myself. I couldn't imagine he would just invent a story like that. And why would Sara call me first thing? Yes we had worked on a number of projects together, but she was very busy. What was going on?

I settled inside myself to request some inner guidance on what this was about. What I heard was, "Perhaps all three of you were lying just a little and hugely embarrassed by that, scrambling to push away the shame with a version of the story that was plausible and presentable." I caught the truth of this.

Then the memory of a childhood event surfaced. I had been discovered doing something considered inappropriate and was shamed for it. The emotional experience of shame is very powerful, like being exposed naked in front of others; being suddenly vulnerable. I could appreciate how strong the impulse would be to cover up inappropriate actions to avoid public humiliation. And immediately I was embarrassed that I had tried to shade the truth with Harry. I let myself know that even people with integrity sometimes shade the truth. Shading the truth might be a behavior I was capable of, but it didn't represent the essence of who I am. Talking with myself as an adult might carefully explain something to child, I made it safe for the inner truth to come forward. I was making it safe to learn.

> **I found my mind stuck on the encounter, looking for the meaning.**

Let me see if I can just get honest with myself about what was going on, I thought. Let me stop telling myself my version of the story and just state what I remember having happened. Doing this felt worthwhile. If I had shaded the truth with my version of the story, and made myself bad about doing that, it would explain why the situation was still bothering me. It would explain why I was ready to pounce on Sara or Harry for similar behavior, to make them wrong for it. And if they had been shamed as I had been as a child (and who hasn't?), then it could explain their versions of what had happened. Even with no more information than this, I was ready to extend compassion to all of us, and as I did so, I felt the slight edge I had on the experience begin to lift.

I then thought about what had happened with an intention of correcting any shading I had added to my version of the story.

I "re-rolled" the experience. My first reaction in seeing Harry had been one of split-second self-satisfaction. He looked surprised. I had been in first class, too, and I remembered thinking that I'd hoped he'd inferred that my business was going well. It embarrassed me to admit that I had gone there, but I had. I let that be all right. Even enlightened people can sometimes want others to see that their business is going well.

I had been nervous about talking with Harry—and the truth was that I usually felt nervous talking with Harry. When he first joined the company, I had spoken to him openly about the strengths and opportunities in the company as I saw them. I concluded sometime later that I might have gone overboard with this and that somehow this openness had made him nervous. Perhaps he hadn't liked that I, an outsider, had had these insights. Conversations with Harry inevitably ended up doing me more harm than good.

As a result, I had judged myself as not having the skills needed to take care of myself in conversations with Harry. In trying to win him over, I inevitably just dug myself in deeper. I had stayed to chat with him because I was still attached to winning him over. I was embarrassed to admit this to myself. Staying to talk was the natural thing to do, but my intention had involved manipulation as its underlying factor, not pleasantry, as I had pretended.

When Harry insisted on knowing what work I was doing, I got angry. My interpretation was that he was hoping to hear that I wasn't doing any work for the company. That would have meant he had gotten his way about our involvement. In truth, we were doing minor projects for the company. My comment to Harry that I was about to start working for Sara implied a big project was about to begin. The truth was she engaged me periodically to think through strategies and issues and we simply had another meeting scheduled. Relating this involvement violated a confidence. So I had stretched the truth a bit and stretched a confidentiality boundary as if to say to Harry, "So there! I *am* working for your company!" It would have been more honest to share my feelings of discomfort with Harry about his consistent focus on my involvement with the company and to let him know also that clients at his company often asked that I not mention work I was doing with them. Or, I could have simply asked him: "Why do you want to know?" It seemed so simple in hindsight.

When Harry had made his final comment about Sara, I had been truly puzzled. But I hadn't taken an emotional dive when he did so, and I honored the part of me that didn't. In the past, a comment like that might have felt like a major wallop.

When Sara called, my first thought was, Oh no, she's calling me to chew me out for mentioning her name in the context of our work for the company. I also knew that there could have been truth in what Harry had said, and that she could have been chagrined on that point.

I recalled how, when Sara called, I had rushed into the conversation with my version of the story, slightly down-playing what I had told Harry, stating it to Sara as 'I told him I bumped into you now and then.'

Again I felt shame for having shaded the truth to protect myself from embarrassment. "For God's sake," I told myself, "I want to write a book on truth-telling in business at some point and look what I'm doing. How can I hold myself up as an expert on something that I don't always do?"

So I let that self-judgment come fully forward, emotions of shame and disappointment in myself. Then I let

them go. I realized I had to make learning okay for myself if I was going to be able to encourage a similar learning orientation in others. Accepting that I had shaded the truth didn't mean what I had done was without consequence, and it didn't mean I approved or agreed with my actions. It meant accepting that I am human.

As I felt free of this self-judgment, I realized the hold it had had on me—and how quick I'd always been in general to suspect others of not telling the truth, of how insistent I was that others always tell me the truth. I could see how the situation would have been simpler and more graceful if there had been greater truth-telling on all sides, but I could also accept that in each moment we are all doing the best we can. The peace that had come from being fully honest with myself would allow greater truth telling. I could see this and was grateful for my willingness to take this step. And, as a result, it didn't so much matter then how others had shaded the truth. That was their business; I had handled mine.

> **I simply accepted that I am human.**

I set an intention to develop business relationships where intimacy and the "microscopic truth" can safely

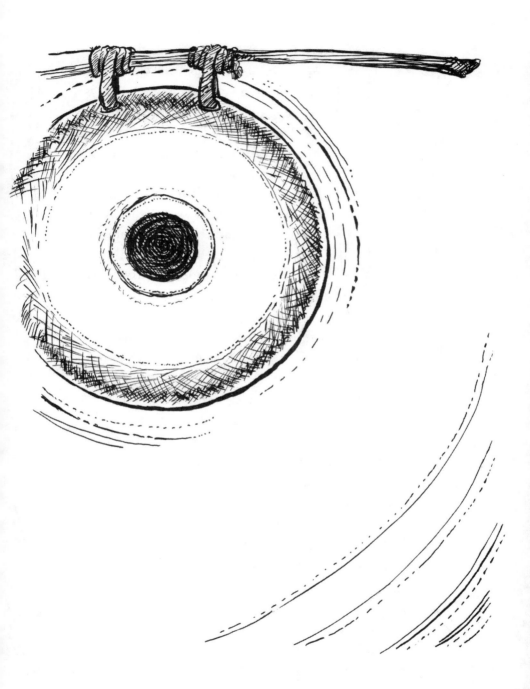

come forward. And I now see that making it safe inside myself to tell myself the microscopic truth about what is happening is the place to start. I also see that to do this, I need to be willing to feel all the feelings that shading the truth is designed to avoid.

To be open to what a situation has to teach us, to learn, we must let go of the position that what has happened is good or bad. That can be a challenge. If I had stayed focused on trying to determine whether Sara or Harry had done anything bad or wrong, I wouldn't have been open to learn what there was for me to learn from the experience. Getting off the position that "what is" is good or bad freed me to look for the learning. And increased intuition is the benefit of being willing to go through life with a learning orientation.

Again, this is not to imply that I am always attuned inwardly and using my intuition. Sometimes I have held back from asking for this support. As I become aware of the "self-talk" in those moments I hear myself saying things like, "You haven't been good lately. You've been too much in your ego, your personality. You don't deserve to receive support. You're not spiritual enough—you're too focused on the task at hand. You better clean up your act first." When I am in this place of self-judgment I can feel like I don't deserve to be supported.

It's so helpful to see self-judgment operating in such a situation, seeing how it creates separation between myself and the greater consciousness of Spirit. To see that I'm the one giving myself the gong. I recognize that at these times, I'm still in my need-approval pattern, but instead of parental or boss approval, I go instead for Spirit's approval. In these times, I don't have so much access to intuition, because I have separated myself from my SELF. I've made *me* more important than Self. But in letting my approval needs go, I become attuned to my learning path and the realization that all is fine—I am just learning.

‡ ‡ ‡

Recently I lost a computer file containing some writing. I suspect that everyone who uses computers has a variety of stories to tell along this line. Usually, I have notes that I use to recreate what disappeared. In this case, however, my writing was in a flow-of-consciousness style whereby I don't really know what I am writing until I've finished when I shift into "mental" mode for editing and fine-tuning. I

> I decided to reach out to the creative consciousness, the energy of Spirit, asking an insight to be present when I awake.

will often write this way when I wake with ideas and feel divinely inspired by my creative consciousness. In this case, I had no recollection of what I had written, just a sense that I had really liked it and I didn't want to let it go.

I stumbled about for a couple of weeks attempting to locate the missing file, bringing in computer software experts, shifting methodically through the recycle/temporary storage bins. Slowly, painfully, I came to the realization that the material was gone. Hearing myself tell myself what I should have done differently to prevent this from happening, I caught myself, seeing that I was making myself wrong. Seeing that I was making what had happened bad.

Disappointment is a challenge. But what we are really saying to ourselves by lamenting loss is that we know that other events, in this case the file not being lost, would have been better. When I was attached to that position, I was unable to ask how come that had happened in a way that invited learning. I was attached to the belief that what happened was bad, and that made the belief true. On the other hand, the supportive way to approach the loss of a job, a project, an employee, a client, a customer, or a file is that some purpose is being served, and to take the opportunity to attune to that purpose. It takes faith to see Spirit as a full partner in this way.

I decided to reach out to the creative consciousness,

the energy of Spirit, which I tap into before bedtime, asking an insight to be present when I awake. "Okay, I'm willing to presume that this was lost in order for some purpose." I said. "But I'd like something better by tomorrow if that is in the greatest good of all concerned." I was on a deadline after all. My tone had softened as I made my wish, not my demand, but my wish.

The next morning I wrote this chapter.

AFTERWORD

*There's no relationship out there. There's only a reflection
of what you're doing inside yourself and how you're
dealing with relationships inside yourself, not out there.*
— JOHN-ROGER

The path to corporate nirvana is about personal
productivity. As we alter our orientation from a right-
wrong model of the world, into a learning model, there are
no mistakes, only wins and learning opportunities. This is
not always easy; it takes faith and courage to see the learning opportunity when we would rather resist learning, by
blaming others (or ourselves) and making what is happening wrong or bad.

In a learning mode, all our energy stays fully focused
on moving toward the goal. Rather than remaining upset,
and using our energy unproductively, in turn lowering the
productivity of others, we lift up and look for the learning,
healing self-judgments and seeing what would work better. In other words, we learn. In this mode, our full creativity, inventiveness, enthusiasm, assets and passion are
engaged as we learn how to reach goals with ever greater
grace and ease.

In taking this path, I keep one thought foremost in
mind: What is the learning? This means seeing how what
is happening "out there" is an opportunity to learn "in
here". It means seeing clearly what is happening, and seeing how it is a gift in support of learning. Since we are all

connected, it means seeing my part in any situation, and taking responsibility to recognize and leverage my learning going forward, and seeing how I can more effectively support others.

The freedom to see the learning, which is really letting go of the belief that I should already know, makes this path an uplifting journey. And from this spirit of gratitude, learning becomes a joyful process of unfolding awareness on how to accelerate productivity toward goals.

Making it Happen

From Judith Anderson:

We have seen the processes outlined in this book work time and again in companies large and small. I would appreciate hearing your stories about how you apply these strategies on the job—how you make work REALLY work by integrating your own learning process.

Please accept my invitation to share your success with me and others who find themselves in tough situations. Simply write up the situation, what you did, how it affected you and others around you, and what you learned.

You certainly don't have to be a great writer, just present the information in a straightforward way. And be sure to let us know whether we can use your name or not by including the following statement with your story: *I give (do not give) permission to use my name with this write-up.* We strictly respect your privacy.

You can send these to me c/o Silver Falls Press, 1680 95th Avenue NE, Salem, OR 97301. Please also visit our website at:

CorporateNirvana.com

I welcome your participation in transforming the environment in more of our companies into a corporate nirvana.

ENGAGE JUDITH ANDERSON FOR YOUR COMPANY

Judith Anderson is an expert in the enlightened approach to accelerating productivity in the corporate environment. She shares her innovative insights with enthusiasm, expertise and eloquence.

She devotes her time to her consulting business, Anderson & Rust, and is a partner in LeadershipU.org, a company that provides leadership education and change management consulting to corporate executives.

In addition to her consulting work, Judith is available for a limited number of speaking engagements and seminars.

She can be reached at:

Tel: 201-236-0503
Fax: 201-934-7426

For additional information, please visit these websites:

LeadershipU.org
AndersonRust.com
CorporateNirvana.com

www.CorporateNirvana.com